The Reflective Mentor: Case Studies in Creating Learning Partnerships

The Reflective Mentor: Case Studies in Creating Learning Partnerships

Alyce Hunter and Henry G. Kiernan

Credits

Christopher-Gordon Publishers, Inc.
1502 Providence Highway, Suite 12
Norwood, MA 02062
800-934-8322

Printed in the United States of America

10 9 8 7 6 5 4 3 2 1   08 07 06 05

Library of Congress Catalog Card Number: 2004115572

ISBN: 1-929024-85-1

Table of Contents

This chapter talks about both informal, or natural, and formal, or planned, mentoring of new teachers. It relates a history of the concept of mentoring. Five specific roles for mentors are identified and analyzed.

As a mentor of mentors, a former director of staff development places mentoring in the context of the professional school community. Specific details, including sample forms and letters, describe the initiation and implementation of a collaborative mentoring program.

A mentor coordinator discusses the design and implementation of her school district's mentoring program. Both philosophical and "hands-on" activities are described.

A school district director provides a comparison between mentoring and orientation in the business world and in schools. Concepts and ideas from business organizations are explained and then applied in the context of schools. Specific "best practices" with regard to mentoring are detailed.

A "new" teacher describes how being mentored has transformed his perception of himself as a teacher, a professional, and a member of a supportive learning community.

Introduction

Perspectives on Mentoring

Alyce Hunter

The Reflective Mentor: Creating Partnerships in Learning is the next step. It goes beyond describing mentor programs and giving advice about how to mentor teachers. It is a book full of real-life stories. Contributions are included by those who have mentored, been mentored, have supervised mentor relationships, and have instituted and run mentor programs. The voices are those of practitioners, researchers, classroom teachers, preservice teachers, experienced educators, professors, and administrators. Additionally, contributors come from a variety of academic disciplines and different geographic areas.

The book concentrates on the fundamental issue of how to improve mentoring practices through concentrating on the belief that new teachers are part of an educational community. Samples of reflective practices are abundant. Each chapter can stand alone as its own unique telling about the ups and downs of mentoring relationships and programs. However, taken all together, the chapters progress from, and complement, each other. The first chapter lays the groundwork for all types of formal and informal mentoring of new teachers. The second chapter places mentoring in the context of the entire school community. Subsequent entries detail and evaluate implementation strategies. Mentors are given practical suggestions about observation strategies. Next, the necessity and complexity for mentoring all educators—including administrators—are emphasized. Finally, the importance of creating a school climate and environment that supports the mentoring program and the subsequent professional development of all educators, is explained.

Section I

Mentoring as a Way of
Teaching and Learning

Chapter 1

The Teacher as Mentor

Ronald T. Sion

Mentor: Myth, Legend, Reality

In Homer's epic poem, *The Odyssey*, the elder friend and advisor of Odysseus was named Mentor, a Greek word meaning *enduring* (Dennis, 1993). The wise counselor was given the responsibility of educating the protagonist's son, Telemachus. But this education was more than academic—in fact, Mentor was responsible for the physical, social, ethical, and moral comportment of the young man. Far more compelling was Mentor's duty to teach the boy how to think and act independently (Young & Wright, 2001). This sounds very much like what modern educators are asked to perform with their students each day.

The word *mentor*, although epic in origin, has nevertheless become an eponym in modern times for a tutor, a coach, a counselor, or a guide. While the relationship between Mentor and Telemachus has rarely been literally duplicated, the story can act as a model in comprehending the mentoring process and its practical application in the education profession (Young & Wright, 2001).

What qualities did Mentor possess that made him so good at what he did? James B. Rowley (1999) suggests that a good mentor must be: (1) committed to the role; (2) accepting of the protégé; (3) skilled at providing instructional support; (4) effective in a variety of interpersonal situations; (5) model the perpetual learner; and (6) communicate optimism (pp. 20–22).

The mentor must also be knowledgeable within his or her field, a good listener, and a keen problem solver (Young & Wright, 2001). Most, if not all, of these qualities can be found in many educators who are: (1) committed to their profession; (2) accepting of their students; (3) skilled at what they do; (4) willing to share with others; (5) have a keen desire to learn; and, (6) most of the time, maintain an optimistic attitude.

Just as Mentor was chosen by Odysseus to guide his son, so, also, are numerous educators chosen daily to guide the youth of the world on the road to learning. What often fails to happen in educational circles, however, is that these same educators, who guide their students so skillfully, do not support each other in the same manner. Without a formal program, model, or invitation in place, educators are reluctant to assume a role to which they are unassigned. Hence, the opportunity for true pedagogical reform and enrichment is missed.

Ironically, the range of a teacher's pedagogical practices often determines whether there will be "180 days of joy or drudgery" in the classroom (Wasley, 1999, p. 8). Encouraged to seek professional development through workshops, graduate courses, or publications, educators often fail to see the rich pedagogical resource that surrounds them—each other. By observing many images of good teaching, a repertoire of instructional strategies can be found that will enhance both educators and students alike (Wasley, 1999).

The teacher, in essence, can be a proactive agent to improve pedagogical practices within his or her own school. This could be the basis for the restructuring of schools with colleagues—both veteran and novice—working together in teams (Tell, 1999). This synergistic, collaborative process could renew the old and encourage the new; it could change the whole working climate within the school. Through collegial support, the weak would be strengthened, the dynamic affirmed, and the neophyte encouraged. It may prove to be the very tool that reduces the dropout rate, diminishes burnout, and, ultimately, abates the teacher shortage.

Open the Door

Within the confines of a historical context—Mentor to Telemachus—it may appear that mentoring is limited to a narrow, structured platform. On the contrary, however, as will be illuminated in this chapter, mentoring has a wide range of possibilities in the world of education.

For example, a student-teaching experience can prove to be more than an internship—it can become the introduction to professional enrichment in the multifaceted and rewarding world of mentoring. If the cooperating teacher is a good mentor, the protégé can learn so much more on the job than any educational textbook could ever supply. But even if the cooperating teacher is a traditionalist who lacks the desire to give fully to the protégé in the hopes of grooming a sound educator for the future, the student teacher has a unique opportunity that may not be afforded later in his or her professional career. An explanation is rendered.

This writer, a secondary English major, was assigned by his university to a rural junior-senior high school and a cooperating teacher who taught only three sections of English (her other two classes were Latin). Pleasant, kind, and in full control of her class, she eased her student teacher into his duties until he had acquired all three of her classes. Then she allowed him to use the other two periods as planning sessions rather than continue to sit in the classroom observing her daily instruction in Latin.

This time, mostly spent in the teacher's lounge, was both intriguing and edifying. Interspersed between the jokesters, the haughty, and the aloof was a group of dynamic, affable educators who were more than willing to share their years of experience with the new kid on the block. Here was a team of mentors offering ideas, responding to questions, and relating amusing anecdotes that would remain with the educator for life. One day, a suggestion was made: "Why don't you visit other classes during your 'free' time?" With the approval of the cooperating teacher, the weeks that followed were a veritable potpourri of pedagogical experiences, many rewarding, some disheartening, but all integral aspects of the mentoring experience.

Some teachers, when approached to observe their class, were highly complimented and gratified by the request, providing lesson plans in advance, and open to discussions both before and after the visit. They even solicited honest evaluations of the novice; some were hesitant, nervous, and slightly defensive: "Why in the world would you want to observe my class—I'm a math teacher, not an English instructor." A few teachers avoided the issue altogether so that their classes were never observed—although, on the record, they never actually refused.

Besides the phenomenal insights gained by observing these veterans, an interesting sidebar occurred: Some of the quietest, least outgoing personalities outside the classroom became dynamos within it. They were alive, charismatic, creative, and student-centered. Conversely, a few of the more outgoing and witty personalities in the teacher's lounge left these attributes at the door and took on a more rigid, businesslike demeanor when in the formal classroom setting. A few—like the 6 ft 3 in physically commanding presence—had no control over the discipline of his class, which made it a painful one to observe. Ironically, a petite 4 ft 11 in maternal veteran held supreme control over her class and mesmerized her students in a warm, positive, and respectful environment. The conclusion: One cannot judge the competency of the teacher either by physical demeanor or personality projected outside the classroom—the personas do not always match.

Several teachers were unnerved by the presence of a visitor, conjuring up the oft-repeated words of a colleague that teaching is a public profession which is done privately—these teachers were only accustomed to the planned, once-a-year visit of an administrator or department chair. Years later, a veteran colleague on the staff would relate how nervous she became whenever these visits were scheduled. One day, a colleague lingered in the computer lab where her class met after its arrival. Nervously approaching the other teacher, she asked him to leave—ostensibly because there were not enough computers to go around. In reality, as she was to admit later, she was too uncomfortable and/or insecure to teach with a coworker present.

John Donne wrote that "no man is an island" (1989, p. 284). In the emotionally charged profession of teaching, these words are prophetic when the school building encourages isolated islands of learning that, collectively, are all part of one process. Rogers & Babinski (1999) write of the establishment of new teaching groups to break down these barriers, in order to alleviate the physical and social isolation often experienced by novices (pp. 38–40).

Educators in general, whether novice, veteran, or anywhere in-between, desperately need each other in an ongoing, nurturing process—far too many burn out or abandon their initial dedication to their craft due to a lack of affirmation, a sense of isolation, and professional stagnation. Whether sharing ideas or opening the classroom door to visitors in formal or informal settings, teachers can guide and enlighten each other. The student-teaching experience described above set this writer on a path that has sustained and enriched him: Open the door—as well as the discussion—to colleagues, for they will stimulate and improve you as an educator. Being open to a diverse and enriching variety of educational experiences will also aid in the development of beneficial mentoring skills.

Key Element for Success

The advising, coaching, and nurturing aspects of good mentoring can only be achieved with the cooperation of both parties. Telemachus played an integral role in the mentoring process: he had to be open to Mentor's instructions. While he may have had an expectation of what Mentor could provide for him, he needed to bring with him an open mind and a desire to learn for the relationship to succeed. The latter is a necessary agent for success within each teacher's classroom every day. Without a cooperative attitude on the part of the student, the teacher may as well be talking to him- or herself—little learning will take place. Likewise, the mentor and mentee must be comfortable with each other—they need not be friends, but they must respect each other professionally (Young & Wright, 2001).

From that point forward, the success of the relationship depends on what each brings to it. The test: Have the needs been met and the goals accomplished (Young & Wright, 2001)? The answer may neither be definitive nor conclusive, since it is a work in progress, but each party is keenly aware, along the way, as to whether the experience is an enriching one that has advanced in the proper direction.

The Teacher in the Heart of the Process: Five Roles

Essentially, mentoring takes on two forms in education: (1) informal, or natural; and (2) formal, or planned. Informal, or natural, mentoring takes place through collegial friendships, coaching, or counseling; formal, or planned, mentoring is a structured process, where mentors and participants are selected and matched (Dennis, 1993). The veteran teacher may, at one time or another, find him- or herself in any of the following five mentoring roles: (1) cooperating teacher; (2) collegial mentors in a team teaching program; (3) peer coaching member; (4) a constructive, uncritical visitor to another educator's classroom; or (5) department chair.

The cooperating teacher finds him- or herself in the unique position to truly mentor a protégé who is new to education. All that this young, impressionable individual sees and hears may be the archetype of a future educator. Although the cooperating teacher may be asked to evaluate the student teacher's performance, never again, in most teachers' careers, do they spend so much time with another educator on the firing line—within the classroom. The full dimension of mentoring responsibility is clearly in the hands of the cooperating teacher/mentor. A positive, affirming, growth-oriented, and nonintimidating relationship is essential for the protégé's culminating training experience to be successful.

When teachers team together, as in an interdisciplinary venture, they end up mentoring each other. Often, a team leader or captain is assigned or elected. Even when this is not the case, the group frequently confers this role to the veteran. While the leader or captain may be regarded as a mentor, he or she invariably shares this role with the other team members. The dynamics of teachers planning and implementing a lesson together inevitably dictates a variety of mentor-protégé sessions. Even an isolated team teaching venture—one in which two or three colleagues get together to create and implement a single multi-disciplinary lesson plan—may accrue mentoring benefits.

Peer coaching—a process whereby teachers team together to improve or enhance their pedagogical techniques—is a planned form of mentoring that contains, within itself, natural elements. The team members may be assigned, or be free to select, members under administrative guidance. In either case, a spirit of collegiality is present when teachers team for the sole purpose of observing, dialoguing, and supporting each other. Although a team captain may also be assigned, he or she takes on a more organizational role than that of mentor, while the process allows for each member to be on both the giving and receiving end of the mentor-protégé experience.

Formal visits to unique programs in other schools, or classrooms within one's own school—limited to a single discipline or across disciplines—is a fourth dimension, in which the benefits of mentoring may be derived. The images of good teaching practices are not earmarked exclusively for any one discipline, or for any one part of the student population. The more one observes, the more ample the opportunities are to add to one's grab bag of instructional techniques.

Although it certainly may be seen as an administrative role, the department chair is presented here as a participant in a formal, or planned, aspect of mentoring. In his or her role, the department chair bears responsibility for the flow and sequence of academic instruction. Generally a veteran who is deemed to be a master teacher, he or she can be an instructional resource for teachers who are new to the system, or to education in general. Likewise, the department chair can act as a coach encouraging collegial support, both within and outside the department, while using the department meeting forum as a vehicle for pedagogical enhancement.

Far too frequently, a new teacher's enthusiasm is enervated by a lack of support—they are left floundering without guidance. Veteran teachers have always been helping beginners, but perhaps not as often, or as intensely, as the beginner might like (Johnson, 2001). The department chair can alleviate this situation; he or she can become an instrumental agent in the retention of good teachers who might otherwise leave the profession out of frustration. Although some may argue that a department chair—in some districts a formal evaluator of a teacher's performance—should, by the very nature of his or job description, be excluded from the mentoring process, it is the contention of this writer that to do so is detrimental to both teacher and chair alike. A department chairperson, endowed with competent mentoring skills, can also be an invaluable mentor.

Five possible mentoring roles exist in the life of a teacher. Each of these vital aspects of mentoring will now be examined in greater detail, with case studies of successes and shortcomings analyzed.

The Cooperating Teacher

Teaching has been a career in which the greatest challenge and most difficult responsibilities are faced by those with the least experience.

—(Glickman, Gordon, & Ross-Gordon, 1998, p. 21)

Anthony Sion was a master plumber. In a tradition that began with his European ancestry, he first worked as an apprentice, learning the tools of the trade until he was promoted to the position of journeyman. Once again, he had to pass the test of time in the front lines before he took a written, practical exam to prove himself worthy of the title of master. Once attained, he achieved both a benefit and a heavy responsibility: first, the option was now available for him to begin his own business independent of supervision; second, he was now obligated as master to teach, train, and nurture new apprentices hired under his care. Watching the master at work, both in the planning and implementation stage of contracted work, the success of the apprentice was dependent on the skill, the capability, and the willingness of the master to dispose of his knowledge to the apprentice learning the trade. Similarly, in this analogy, the initial test of the apprentice is administered by the cooperating (master) teacher in the field of education.

The cooperating teacher acts as a master in imparting his or her skill to the novice educator. This new teacher's primary success is dependent on two conditions: (1) the degree of innate talent with which he or she is endowed, interfaced with the interpersonal skills attained in working with young minds; and (2) the nurturing of this intrinsic ability in spring training camp under the demonstrable guardianship of a skillful, knowledgeable, and seasoned professional. The fusion of inherent talent with the guidance of a generous, enthusiastic virtuoso will, over time, erupt into a combustible, dynamic journeyman who is well on his or her way to eventual mastership.

The student teacher needs to be carefully mentored through his or her apprenticeship before assuming status as a full-time teacher under a department chair. The cooperating teacher, therefore, undertakes a critical, profound, and meaningful role in sculpting a future educator. The cooperating teacher must be a collaborator who critically, but constructively, supports the novice educator to plan, to teach, to ponder, and to apply new scholarship into practice.

The cooperating teacher is the student teacher's first mentor. He or she introduces the mentee for the first time to the full spectrum of teaching duties—from planning to implementation, from assessment to reflection. Pre- and post-conferences, both before and after the experience, are crucial; candid appraisals, in introspect, are invaluable; affirmation as well as constructive criticism, in context, is essential. Hopefully, all will nurture the young educator and provide an occasion for growth. The cooperating teacher must be more than the one who provides the grade, to determine if the student teacher will graduate—in many ways, he or she is the determining factor as to whether the student teacher will continue to pursue a teaching vocation.

Jill was that rare commodity—she had an innate ability, a thorough knowledge of subject matter, and a keen desire to work creatively with young minds. Yet, despite all her bravado, she was insecure. She desperately needed support and affirmation. Her cooperating teacher was more than willing to stand aside, let her experiment with new pedagogical approaches, and be an audible cheering section to her accomplishments. She would have been a competent teacher without guidance; but she was an assured, remarkable teacher with it.

Mark tried so hard to be "cool" that he forgot he was the teacher and not one of the students. Although he was only a few years older than the seniors he taught, it was crucial for his cooperating teacher to point out to him where he was headed—a turbulent sea, where he would capsize and be unable to keep his head above water. She spoke openly to Mark, but allowed him to experience some elements of discomfort before interceding. She asked him to review the rationale behind the protocol she demanded, and received, from her students. In a candid discussion, he realized that respect, kindness, and affirmation could be generated, while still maintaining a warm teacher-student separation. In short order, Mark was able to retain his "cool" label without undermining his role as teacher.

As a mentor gives freely to a mentee, so also, in return, he or she receives so much. For the cooperating teacher has the unique ability to step back once more and recount his or her first teaching experience. Once again, by stepping into the shoes of the protégé, they see their profession anew. And so it is that one is so profoundly renewed by the experience. How special can these moments be when one sees the future passed on to the new generation that will follow after his or her retirement? Every teacher should be a cooperating teacher at least once in his or her professional career. What a rich heritage there is, ready to be passed on to a dynamic, refreshing new generation of educators!

The Team Member: Collegial Mentors

Nine years ago, an interdisciplinary team-taught program of study was implemented at the school where I then served as English department chairperson. I left my authority as chair, however, at the door and joined the team as an equal member. Despite the fact that I had been teaching for well over 12 years at the time, I was about to embark on a new venture that would enhance my perspective of mentoring.

For organizational purposes, a team working together, either formally or informally, appoints a chair or team leader. As a veteran, I accepted the position but also removed myself from any evaluative role. Whether or not a leader is selected, however, does not change the dynamics: When teachers are "forced" to work together, they end up (for better or worse) mentoring each other. This is especially true if the team of teachers is present in the same classroom at the same time, which was the case in this interdisciplinary approach.

Interdisciplinary instruction requires that teachers either see through the lens of the other discipline or at least make the connections between disciplines (Jacobs, 1989). In order to do so, colleagues need to respect each other professionally and have a sincere regard for what the other has to offer to the class in the attainment of the lesson's goals. Sharing the same space, they need to reflect a respectful, cooperative attitude toward each other, both in front of and behind the scenes, and share their expertise in the design and implementation of classroom activities and assessments. In short, they are in a working relationship that emulates a professional marriage.

The team meetings can prove to be both stimulating and frustrating—stimulating when new ideas are generated and the team members pitch in to bring them to fruition; frustrating when members cannot see eye-to-eye or when some members refuse to pull their weight in carrying out projects. This is when the leadership skills of the team leader are challenged.

Jim, Sally, and Judy were my partners in three successive years. Each brought different personality traits, life experiences, and professional attributes to our partnerships. Each was the social studies component that was to blend with me, the English component, in this interdisciplinary venture. While Jim was in his second year of teaching, this was Sally's first; Judy was a veteran, by comparison. Jim was laid-back but very much an idea man—we spent many hours after school and at workshops engaged in stimulating conversations that resulted in a thematic shift to our units. Sally was unsure of herself, and was more than willing to have me take total control—this may have proven comfortable for me, but it stymied her from realizing her full potential. While Judy was cooperative and stable, her teaching style was very traditional and orderly. As I was adjusting to each, they were also adjusting to me.

As an "A" type personality—fastidiously organized, used to be being in control, and department chair—I was challenged to share time and space with others. Additionally, I had to be open to other's ideas, even if I had a strong opinion as to their relative merit. I also had to bite my lip hard and not say "I told you so" when it did not work. Moreover, I had to be willing to bend and state that I was wrong by complimenting others when an approach with which I did not agree succeeded. The unique and unusual aspect of this arrangement was that each member, at one time or another, assumed the role of Mentor as well as Telemachus. On given days, and in the context of the lesson, the roles often interchanged.

Jim appreciated seeing his ideas take shape and form in my hands; I willingly released some control to Sally and affirmed her creative ventures; and Judy became the stabilizing ballast when my approaches went amuck. Jim and I were to bring our ideas to a regional conference as presenters, a concept that I would never have thought of doing alone; I was amazed when Sally created a physical map of South America, with students moving around the room as designated locations; and Judy became an expert on origami when we studied Japan and its art. Jim and I were to implement an Architectural Fair that has been a class event each year, and is still operating today; Sally was open to experimentation: she taught a novel while I swapped places with her in teaching a social studies unit. And Judy was to succeed in obtaining a Humanities grant for travel to Russia, thereby richly enhancing her presentation of that culture's art and history.

Jim was to obtain his master's degree in administration and is now the principal of a charter school; Sally is now editing educational textbooks; and Judy is still a team member, although now partnered with someone else. We all have maintained lasting relationships that have endured over time and distance. Ideally, each teacher should have the opportunity, at one time, to team with another. It is truly a unique mentoring experience that can only foster growth.

Peer Coaching: Colleagues Mentoring Each Other

One simple way for providing a forum, whereby educators can mentor each other, is peer coaching. Several years ago, the vice principal obtained a grant and presented, at the opening faculty meeting of the school year, a voluntary peer-coaching program. We were introduced to the basic tenets of this approach: a team of teachers working together to enhance pedagogical skills. Teachers signed up, teams were devised, and, once more, another vehicle for dissolving isolation and fostering a collaborative environment was implemented.

Besides another teacher within my discipline (English), there was also a math, a science, a social studies, and a modern language teacher on our team. We met initially under the auspices of the vice principal, who then appointed one of us to serve as a moderator or team leader. In addition to informal monthly meetings in which we shared our ideas and related classes that we had observed during the month, there was a verbal commitment that we would try to visit each other's classes at least once in each semester.

Since this was taking place across the disciplines, there was some apprehension; for example, the first time that the math and science teacher visited my classroom or I visited theirs. But once the ice was broken, it generated nothing but positive feedback. Here now were colleagues affirming each other not just within their own areas of specialization, but across the disciplines. New cooperative ventures were generated, including a writing-across-the-curriculum experiment. Ideas were shared that may never have materialized in another forum. Pedagogical approaches were swapped; incredibly, what worked in math or science could actually work in English, and vice versa.

Reasonable expectations had to be set by the team members in advance. What did we hope to accomplish? We started off simple. First, if we achieved nothing else but the experience of seeing what went on across disciplines in the school and saw the world, albeit briefly, through our students' eyes, we would be enriched. Second, we would make an effort to affirm each other through the experience of our visitations. Third, if the teacher being observed requested it, we could act as nonintimidating, objective observers to assist the teacher in getting a better handle on what was taking place within the classroom. And last, we would act as mentors to each other in sharing pedagogical strategies. There was not one member of the team who did not function in all four capacities at least once throughout the classroom visitations.

The roles of mentor and mentee frequently became blurred. What role did I assume when I visited a classroom or was observed? Would I dare to assume that I was a mentor when I visited a math class? Or, was I really a protégé learning from the teacher in another discipline? It was in the feedback and reaction to what went on in the classroom that practical pedagogical learning took place. An aloof, segregated attitude between, and among, disciplines was replaced by one of admiration, respect, and collegiality. Morale was richly endowed by this approach.

Sadly, the peer-coaching model is no longer operating at the school. What happened to it? Why was it not sustained? Did it no longer have value? The irony is that this highly successful and inspiring approach to teachers sharing mentoring roles died due to a change in administration and not out of a lack of interest on the part of team members. Once there was no one in charge offering the approach, it ceased to survive. As is often the case, if leadership is not present to promote, to encourage, and to sustain a concept, its life is frequently threatened. Peer coaching is an extremely worthwhile aspect of professional development, and is truly a mentoring role that all educators can assume. Like everything else in education, however, it needs ongoing nourishment to survive.

Sharing the Wealth

Almost any gathering can turn into a collective of one, a unified field, pure awareness—one richly ordered mind yielding a profusion of novel answers.

—(Sinetar, 1998, p. 143)

Even without a peer-coaching model in place, the wealth between and among educators can be shared both outside and within the school community. Before the interdisciplinary program mentioned above was devised, we did some research and visited several other schools that had unique programs in place. Contact was generally made first to the principal and through him or her to the department chairs.

The department chair at Rogers High School in Newport, Rhode Island, for example, spent well over an hour with me describing her program of study and sharing photocopied materials; teachers at the Algonquin Regional High School in Northborough, Massachusetts, provided a full description, as well as copies of their curriculum and syllabus. In turn, when several years later a local high school planned on developing an interdisciplinary program, they spent the day with us—we reciprocated the kindness that we had received. Last year, we visited a local school to gain insights about our Academic Foundations course of study for basic-level students by observing what they did with that segment of their population. Finally, when our interdisciplinary program was up for review under a new administration, we were observed by a visitor from another school. There is no limit to the enrichment of content, sequence, and approach of instruction that can be gained by visiting other schools and opening one's doors to visitors.

Once again, realistic expectations must be set in advance. The purpose in visiting another school is not to support an elitist attitude that *we* are better, but to interact and share strategies. Although what I have cited were visitations for the express purpose of exploring new programs, there is no reason why, either within or outside school systems, an opportunity could not exist for teachers to observe each other's classrooms as a mentoring model to improve teaching strategies.

More convenient to this approach, however, is the sharing of interdepartmental ventures within one's own school. These can be formally generated through department chairs, or they can come about as a grassroots effort on the part of teachers. In the first instance, for example, I invited the social studies department, on several occasions, to be guests at our English department meetings. The purpose: an open forum to explore what we can do together. Two results: (1) an interdisciplinary, team-taught venture labeled Humanities: American Studies; and, (2) the interdepartmental teaching and assessment of a research paper. In addition, English teamed with another department in the creation and testing of a summer reading list.

In the grassroots arena, I have witnessed the spark of an idea germinated over lunch in the teachers' lounge. For example, the English and drama teachers got together to have their students dramatically render *The Rime of the Ancient Mariner* on videotape; the Charleston was taught to students studying the Roaring Twenties; and the English and social studies teachers worked as a team in generating the concept of *apartheid* outside of the classroom. What does all of this have to do with mentoring?

One of the principal responsibilities of any good mentor in education is to "stretch" the mentee so that they may learn from their experiences. Practical instruction materializes when the mentor is able to share successful strategies with the protégé. But even an excellent mentor, despite how long they have been in education, has limitations to his or her repertoire. If mentoring is expanded to include all teachers in all disciplines, not only within one's school but in other schools, this sharing of the wealth can only enhance, enrich, and expand the instructional lives of all those involved.

Department Chair: The Mentor as Model

While the cooperating teacher may move the student teacher along to the accreditation as a journeyman, it is under the tutelage of the department chair that the new teacher will spend most of his or her time in learning the trade. Some department chairs will serve as little more than a rubber stamp, shuffling the papers of observation with little to no legitimate contact with the amateur—in this case, either additional innate talent or the assistance of colleagues is necessary to improve the quality of the teacher. Whether during chance meetings in the hallways or discussions during common planning periods, experienced educators can act as lifesavers to novices without formal mentors (Delgado, 1999).

Sadly, at least 30% of beginning teachers leave the profession during the first two years (Casey & Mitchell, 1996). Harlan R. Johnson (2001) writes:

> The realities of teaching cannot be grasped through preservice classes and student teaching . . . support and assistance must continue throughout the first year and become part of an ongoing program of professional development (p. 47).

Hence, many department chairs (if they take the job seriously) recognize the tremendous obligation they hold in molding new educators and providing life-giving sustenance to veterans. This is the challenging, and enriching, duty of a master department chair mentor.

For the department chair has been on the job for a significant period of time, he or she knows the ins and outs of the system—how much time can be saved and effort diminished by a few words of wisdom and advice. Moreover, if the department chair still loves what he or she does, then the lessons learned can be shared to such a degree that educators new to the profession or the system can be motivated in ways that are immeasurable.

For example, a colleague turned to his department chair once to ask how he could possibly cover what seemed to be so vast a syllabus in one academic year. After a brief review of the teacher's lesson plans, the chair/mentor offered a suggestion. In his classes, he would frequently assign a novel to be read independently by students while they were reading aloud and discussing a play daily in the classroom. In this way, two major works could be covered concurrently. Likewise, grammar exercises could be practiced for homework while a drama was read in class. By simply providing an example of what the department chair had been doing for years, the teacher—in this case a veteran—was able to implement a new solution to an old dilemma.

Likewise, if a teacher is made to feel that he or she can openly relate their own personal classroom challenges to the chair without judgment or recrimination, then a collegial relationship can develop, with the aim of resolving any issue. Both parties will benefit from such a relationship. Wicks (2000) suggests that, under mentoring lessons, the relationship should be "safe enough for people to share intense feelings" (p. 130).

For example, a teacher candidly offered that she was having discipline problems in her basic-level class. After discussing the situation at length and observing the classroom, the chair/mentor was able to suggest some simple solutions, such as: (1) changing the seats of the disruptive students; (2) issuing doable consequences; and (3) ultimately looking for signs as to when to request administrative and/or parental assistance. In short order, the problem was alleviated, the teacher was once more enjoying the class, and the students were the beneficiaries.

A first-year, young, dynamic, student-centered teacher joined the staff—the department chair considered him to be a delight to have onboard, since his enthusiasm was infectious. Some veterans within the department, however, were less than supportive of his ideas as expressed at meetings. The young man literally pulled back into his shell when criticized about his suggestion that students create a collage as part of an assessment. The chair spoke up at the meeting in his defense. Addressing the teacher who criticized the suggestion, he asked, "Is there anything wrong with John's suggestion? Does it lack academic or instructional value?" The teacher's response was, "Well, maybe it does have value, but don't expect me to assign *my* students a collage." Pointing out that the concept was fine, the chair diplomatically replied, "I can't see you doing this either, Virginia— it would not suit your teaching persona. No one is saying that you need to implement this approach, but in an open-minded environment of collegial support, can't you see that it fits John to a tee?" She nodded her head in agreement. "John," he continued, "I think it is fine—why not go for it?" John smiled in appreciation, and now realized that even his ideas—the ideas of a novice—would be heard.

The department chair whose door is always open, and who warmly encourages educational dialogue with his or her members, may serve as an advisor who listens attentively, thereby affirming pedagogical experimentation and reducing isolation on the part of the teacher. An example of this model can be heard in the words of a recent colleague, who shouted when her department chair returned from maternity leave, "It is so nice to have someone once again who I can bounce ideas off of."

The chair as mentor—if approachable, supportive, and uncritical—may be a teacher's primary liberator in a day sometimes marked by personal and professional challenges. There is not a single person—administrator or colleague— who a novice teacher turns to more often for advice, guidance, clarification, and direction than a department chair. This is true not only in areas of instruction and/or content, but also in personal affirmation. The soundness of the professional mentoring association that the chair develops with his or her protégé/member will determine the success of such a relationship.

When, recently, a teacher had a heated discussion with an administrator over a policy issue, her chair, present for a portion of the meeting, noted how visibly upset his colleague was. Escorting her to the class that immediately followed, the chair insisted on staying with the students in the classroom while his colleague spent some quiet time removed from the scene to recover her composure. Thankful for the kind gesture, the teacher, however, indicated in the corridor that she would resign at the end of the day. The chair insisted that they talk this through before making such a rash, emotionally charged decision. At day's end, the chair met with her and, after a lengthy, open discussion, all was well and no resignation was tendered. The chair also acted as a liaison, interceding on the teacher's behalf to the administrator the following day. Subsequently, the disagreement was dissolved.

Not only can the department chair act as a liaison for the teacher with the administration, but he or she can also be a convenient vessel of diplomatic, rational wisdom in dealing with parents and other colleagues. Following the pattern of Mentor with Telemachus, the chair can assist the protégé in not just the academic or instructional aspects of education, but also in the physical, social, ethical, and moral compartment of a teacher's daily experiences.

Seeds for Growth: Three Reflective Personal Experiences

Not every mentoring venture is as successful, but each experience, even if less than exemplary, has within it the seeds for growth. To that end, three reflective personal experiences are offered here. All three cited examples have common threads: (1) in each case, the woman was in her first year of teaching; (2) an aspect of the major instructional challenge was classroom management; and (3) the mentor-mentee relationship floundered. Perhaps the greatest lesson learned by the mentor was that, no matter how hard one tries, one cannot will a "perfect" teacher the way Pygmalion molded his perfect woman and brought her to life. Nor is this goal appropriate or realistic. Likewise, "a mentor is mortal and, as such, imperfect" (Sinetar, 1998, p. 141). Hence, no matter how seasoned the professional, there is still much to learn when it comes to establishing and sustaining a relationship with the protégé.

Jessica had only been offered a one-year contract. Her colleagues, who taught in adjoining rooms, frequently voiced their complaints about the chaos in her classroom to me, her chair, but never directly to her. When I observed her class, everything was fine—the students were well behaved, mainly because a third party was present. Jessica refused to accept ownership of her problem and consistently pretended that all was okay, despite evidence to the contrary, when one simply walked down the corridor and witnessed the noise emitting from her classroom. Perhaps she was frightened of my authority or what her admission of a "weakness" might mean to her assessment; perhaps I came across as too strong a "boss" who lacked the compassion to listen to her concerns. Maybe the fact that she was only hired for one year destroyed her motivation. Nonetheless, when suggestions were made, she would just nod her head in agreement, but there was always an uncertainty that she was truly listening. An impenetrable wall began to be erected between us—a wall that could not be scaled, no matter how hard one tried to engage her in meaningful dialogue.

One day, observing a teacher next door, I and the students in the room were distracted by the noise in the adjoining computer laboratory, where Jessica taught a writing class. Students were shouting, singing, and even running around, a fact that could be observed through the glass wall separating the rooms. Only occasionally could one discern Jessica's voice, but it was obviously difficult for her to be heard above the din. I probably broke every rule of protocol and exacerbated an already tenuous relationship by leaving the classroom where I was seated and entering into the adjoining room. I was definitely motivated to substantiate what I knew had been taking place within Jessica's classes. I responded, therefore, by berating her students for their disrespectful behavior in front of their teacher.

I did sincerely apologize to her for my behavior after the incident; however, I was trusting that something positive might come out of my less-than-appropriate reaction. This event, however, only made matters worse. Instead of seeing this as an opportunity to open up to me and to express her candid difficulty in keeping order in the classroom (an admission that might have allowed us to work together toward a reciprocal good), Jessica continued on a defensive stratagem. First, she offered that the students really weren't all that bad; second, she noted that she was unaware that their voices were disturbing anyone nearby; and third, since it was late in the day, they were just having a little fun.

The one-year contract was offered as a safeguard due to personnel shifts, so Jessica did not need to have a reason for not being rehired. If the relationship had proved different, perhaps I might have petitioned the powers that be to keep her employed at the school. At any rate, I wrote her a generic letter of recommendation, but felt that I had failed her completely. Whether reviewing her assessments, examining lesson plans, or attempting to engage her in discussions of pedagogy, I was helpless—only silence or a nodding head was returned. I could not penetrate the veneer until, eventually, I stopped trying.

In retrospect, maybe Jessica was responding in a silent manner that said, "You will not enter my domain" until the fateful day that I did so in the worst possible manner. Although I scolded the students, I might as well have admonished her. Perhaps Jessica was saying, "I will not regard you as a mentor." If so, I wish that I had openly expressed to her my vexation at her lack of responsiveness rather than having it erupt in this way. If Jessica had been forthright with me before this incident, would I have reacted in the same manner? I think not, and therein lies the gist of the matter. I am not sure if Mentor always did everything correctly; nor am I satisfied that Telemachus was always responsive. But I am certain that they needed to respect each other. I know now that Jessica's ongoing, silent manner affected me so much that I no longer reflected to her that I respected her as a person, let alone as a teacher. Perhaps this is what she was picking up on and returning to me through her continuing silence.

In an interview with *Educational Leadership,* Asa Hilliard indicates that the most important quality of a good teacher is the ability to relate to students as human beings (Checkley & Kelly, 1999). So, also, do the mentor and mentee need to acknowledge and respect the personal integrity of each other. Maybe another person as department chair/mentor may have succeeded—I know that, for me, this was an excruciatingly bitter experience. If I had to do it over again, I might have tried soliciting the aid of a third party—it certainly might not have hurt, considering how things turned out. While neither of us were effective or respectful communicators, Jessica and I needed to revisit the basis of our mentor-mentee relationship to openly determine what we both hoped to achieve before it reached a crescendo.

David E. and Toni A. Campbell indicate that a recent approach to studying the mentor-mentee relationship is to view it as a dyadic exchange. As such, each openly enters the relationship with specific needs, expectations, and assumptions. Conflict results, however, as it did with Jessica, when these expectations are not achieved (Campbell & Campbell, 2000). Both Jessica and I needed to stop somewhere along the way to reexamine our goals—perhaps then we may have advanced on an appropriate and rewarding path.

In the second scenario, Alice was hired the day before school began due to a resignation on the very day of teacher orientation. The administration was keenly motivated to get someone in the classroom on opening day. Hence, despite the fact that she had no teaching experience, they hired her on an emergency basis. Now the expediency of their decision making became my yearlong enigma. Eventually, Alice resigned at the conclusion of the third quarter, and the department (including myself) took on extra classes to accommodate the students until year's end. What happened?

Alice had attended a teacher's college but never took a practicum in student teaching. Majoring in English, her grades were borderline. Consequently, the school would not officially admit her into the secondary education program. Her father was an educator, and Alice wanted so badly to please him that she rushed headlong into a full-time teaching position inadequately prepared.

Grades aren't everything, and some of the best practicing educators were not necessarily outstanding scholars when they were in school. Sometimes their own lack of interest as students generates imaginative lesson plans as teachers that peaks the attention of diverse ability groups. In Alice's case, however, it was not just the lack of good grades in her academic major that hampered her performance, but the lack of pedagogical training—she did not know how to create and implement a lesson plan.

Through frequent observations and, more particularly, the dialogue that followed, progress was made. Alice was guided to evaluate herself and uncover resolutions to a complex of difficulties that she was experiencing. It was determined, however, that the students were suffering during their teacher's learning curve. Lagging far behind in the syllabus, practically 90% of Alice's students had A's, and some 20%, incredibly, achieved grades of 100. She was a kind and generous person, but not yet a teacher. Ultimately, a question had to be phrased and an answer sought: Were her students really learning? Upon close examination, the response was negative when coupled with her inability to control classroom discipline. Disastrous results ensued. Students complained to guidance counselors; parents called; the administration was forced to intrude on a chaotic classroom setting; and, eventually, Alice—on an emotional treadmill—was relieved when she was encouraged to resign.

I made every attempt to honor the personal integrity of Alice and always treated her with respect and concern. A support group (i.e., her two department chairs, an administrator, and a colleague) was formed to assist her. The best mentoring I could provide in this situation, however, was to ultimately encourage Alice to return to school to get the training that she had missed.

In hindsight, I should have been more assertive with the administration in the hiring process. Perhaps a few mentoring skills should have been invoked in my interaction with them, since they pushed for her employment under impossible circumstances—being hired the day before school opens, with no teacher training, is an accident waiting to happen. I believe that the school performed a disservice to Alice, as well as to the students entrusted to her care, in hiring her.

Department chairs can mentor innate ability that is blended with knowledge and training. But if one is missing, there is little one can do. I am pleased to report that Alice has returned to school; hopefully, she will soon be back in the classroom with a new perspective on teaching rooted in a firmly prepared foundation.

The third narrative focuses on Caitlin, a woman in her early thirties. She had an 8-year-old daughter and had been a stay-at-home mom since the child's birth. She returned to school a couple of years earlier to attain her education credits, and only had substitute as well as student-teaching experience. Caitlin was recently divorced, insecure, and vulnerable. Hired early in the summer months, I had never met her, and had just assumed the duties of department chair 2 weeks before the opening of school. At our initial meeting, I observed that she spoke very loud, interrupted others, and displayed far more than what could be termed first-year jitters.

Caitlin was at my door daily with questions and concerns; every afternoon she would ask to meet with me. Her classes were less than models of discipline, and, frankly, she did not know how to respond to the students. I tried to explain to her how important it was to be meticulously organized, how it was essential that a first-year teacher set reasonable classroom policies, with realistic consequences for violators. Half of her students were failing at the quarter, many complained that the assessments had little relationship to the material covered, and they also protested that they were unable to learn in such a noisy, disorganized environment. More importantly, Caitlin found it increasingly more difficult to maintain her composure, screaming louder and louder above the turmoil, slamming the door, and crying both in the classroom and at our meetings.

Caitlin and I began to work on a plan. First, I guided her through a lesson plan and assisted her in creating appropriate assessments. I visited the classroom more frequently and worked on a plan of action for overall discipline. The vice principal of student life also assisted in this domain. The greatest challenge, however, was not in these areas but in Caitlin's perception of herself. The anger she harbored for her ex-husband and the roller-coaster ride she was now experiencing in a new relationship were contributing to a persona that often appeared on the verge of a breakdown. Although I tried to truly listen to Caitlin, encouraged her to learn from her failures, and tried to interject some humor in the situation, she was asking me to move into personal areas that required more psychological than mentoring care.

Caitlin began to wear the same clothes to school each day—they were wrinkled and stained. Her physical appearance was unkempt, and these were seen as areas that her mentor/chair did not feel he had the professional right to enter. Recommendations were made through others who occasionally socialized with her, and some school services tried diplomatically to assist with her personal baggage. It was determined in March, however, that her contract would not be renewed, which made the balance of the school year even more trying.

I agree that a mentor needs to assume a variety of different roles, including: "role model, teacher, motivator, communicator, resource person, counselor, supporter, advisor, talent developer, guide, demonstrator, and protector" (McKenna, 1998, p. 49).

But this mentor knows his limitations when the counseling role delves into matters of personal concern and emotional stability. Catlin did not request, nor did I agree in the negotiation of our mentoring relationship, to assist her in personal relationships outside of the school. Caitlin did not request, nor did I agree, to protect and defend her emotional stability on the job that was resulting from matters exclusive of the educational circle. Eccentricity may be the vanguard of dynamic personalities and intelligent minds, but when it interferes with the ordinary ability to perform one's duties, even the most compassionate, well-trained department chair knows that the mentee's expectations go beyond his or her domain.

Despite this rationale, it still hurts when one does not succeed. This was my first year as chair. Would I handle matters differently today? Perhaps. But Caitlin needed professional help, for which I was sorely ill prepared. In addition, where does a mentor draw the line in a relationship? If a mentor-mentee need not be friends, they certainly are not required to be confidants to each other in personal matters outside of their professional environs. Perhaps a more seasoned department chair may have been better able to assist Caitlin, although the results may have been the same.

It was within the on-the-job capacity as department chair that it became crystal clear to me that most teachers—regardless of titles or positions—have had little to no training in formal mentoring. Although some of the tools for good mentoring are identical to those of good teaching, most mentors teach, and have a full slate of, responsibilities while they are asked to mentor. These three experiences keenly necessitated a retooling on my part. Hence, I was to pick up as many books and articles on the subject as I could find, and to also seek advice through an omnipresent, invaluable resource—my colleagues. An effective mentoring relationship is essential to the process. A mentor's preparation for, and sustenance of, the relationship is also crucial (Zachary, 2001).

A Department Chair's Mentoring Role at Department Meetings

Ultimately, the department chair not only assumes a mentoring role one-on-one, but also in the more collective arena of department meetings. He or she may be the agent to inspire others to share pedagogical successes and failures with each other. In an open, synergistic workshop atmosphere, dynamic teaching strategies may result that may not find their appropriate place in any other school forum.

For example, several years ago at a secondary urban high school, it was established, as part of the agenda at monthly English department meetings, that colleagues should come prepared to share a successful teaching strategy with each other. The chair was always ready to model this arrangement by going first.

This function produced a plethora of successful interactive instructional strategies, including: (1) how to teach vocabulary; (2) a "poetry alive" concept; (3) a more definitive research-paper approach; and (4) a lively debate forum that is student-centered. One year alone a Poetry Slam was organized and implemented through a simple question: "What can we do to celebrate National Poetry Month?"

More significantly, through this forum, members have invited each other to observe experimental strategies within their classrooms. Once these colleagues enter each other's classes, isolation is broken down and collegial affirmation is engendered. How enriching it is to hear colleagues singing the praises of each other in a "public" forum at the next departmental meeting. Imitation is regarded as the highest form of flattery. Does anyone realize what it means to an educator to have colleagues ask questions about a new pedagogical approach that he or she created, and then to witness positive feedback when others implement these same ideas? When this happens, colleagues truly become supportive mentors to each other.

As a facilitator who affirms the openness of department members to work with each other toward a common goal, the chair may prove to be a quiet instrument of educational reform within one's school. At the very least, he or she may enrich the professional working environment and provide sustained enthusiasm for the *what*, the *why*, and the *how* of teaching.

Preface to an Epilogue

Several years ago, I started to use a journal to assist me in reflecting upon my teaching experiences. This journal was to act as a guide, enabling me to review the ordinary practices of my daily life to assist in improving my teaching. Perhaps not innovative in concept (Hole & McEntee, 1999), the form was uniquely my own. While culling through the entries, I came across three that are noteworthy for their insights into the teacher as mentor. I hereby provide explanations of each, with the lessons learned and the reflections from the journal interspersed among them.

Three Pages from a Mentor's Journal

1. The cooperating teacher as mentor

Jim was a student at the very university where I was working, part-time, on my doctorate. He was young (21 years old), articulate, made a good first impression, and appeared confident, although understandably anxious, as he accompanied me on his first day as my student teacher. I had spent a couple of hours, several weeks before Jim's arrival, providing him with a tour of the school, copies of the texts we would be using in the Humanities and English classes that were part of my teaching schedule, as well as a curriculum guide for each class. I answered Jim's specific questions about the classes he would eventually be teaching and welcomed him to the school on his first day.

Jim was courteously introduced to the students in each class. I detected immediately that these scholars were impressed with how young he was, as compared to their standard-bearer—nothing makes a veteran teacher feel his or her age more than when one mentors a student teacher. Other than the initial introductions and brief meetings after class, I purposely did not plan anything special for Jim, since I wanted him to witness the ordinary routine of a school day, from homeroom through the class changes. I even encouraged him to attend department and faculty meetings after school hours.

For the first few weeks while Jim observed me teaching, I would hold sessions (at least one per day) in which I would ask him to take note of the variety of pedagogical techniques I was utilizing in the various classes. These techniques included cooperative learning modes, a student-centered pattern, a question-and-answer motif, a student-to-student activity, and so forth. I would also question Jim as to the specific intelligences that I had targeted through the different methodologies, such as kinesthetic, verbal/linguistic, and visual/spatial. I invited him to examine the various assessment tools I was using, from oral and written reports to listening checks, as well as traditional tests.

At the end of the first week, I asked Jim to pretend that he was going to teach a specific class the following day and for homework to prepare for that class, picking up the plan where we had concluded. He was to create an actual lesson plan with objectives, goals, activities, and assessments. After reviewing this with him and finding that he was ready to begin a gradual introduction into instruction, I asked Jim to take over only a segment of one of my classes the following week. This was to be a one-step-at-a-time approach, and it continued over the next few weeks. I never left Jim alone in the classroom—I was always present observing him. It took more than 6 weeks for me to release my entire teaching schedule to him—one class at a time. I still held on, however, to my Advanced Placement (AP) English class, never really releasing the entire class to him but operating in a team-teaching mode for this one section.

During this time, I regularly dialogued with his university secondary program director about Jim's strengths and weaknesses. I was never shy about calling Jim to task in our meetings, if what went on in class was determined not to be sound pedagogy. This determination came about, however, through a dialogical process after the class. I listened attentively as Jim critiqued his lessons and their implementation, and encouraged him when he came up with his own ideas for improvement. I made it a point not to lecture or browbeat Jim—after all, he was a student teacher, and I observed that he was truly trying his best.

This was my first experience as a cooperating teacher. The lessons and insights learned from this experience were edifying. They include:

1. Accepting the responsibility of being a cooperating teacher means more work and not less, if one regards this as a serious mentoring obligation. The time spent with Jim during the school day basically took away all of my free time, so that I took more work home each night than before his arrival. Preparation time, for me, was greater, since I needed to always be well prepared (i.e., I had a constant observer and could not fake it). When I turned a portion of the class over to Jim, I had to coordinate with him, thereby preparing more than an entire class (i.e., his section, my

section, and the integration of our components). Jim and I had to spend time coordinating our grading rubrics and procedures—it would not be fair to the students in these classes to be introduced to an entirely new grading formula. Assessments that Jim prepared needed to be reviewed before they were administered, and the grading of papers needed also to be examined until I was comfortable with his competency. The sessions with his university director were also after school, and the multitude of reports to file during and after Jim's tenure were very time-consuming.

Journal Reflection: I often think back to the days when my friends told me of their student-teaching experiences: Their "critic teacher" (the term previously used) just dumped them into the classroom to sink or swim while they enjoyed a work-free semester. Perhaps this pattern can still be found in some schools, but true mentors would never allow themselves such a dangerous luxury, no matter how competent the young educator. If I were not always in the classroom (not getting into the legal liabilities of such an act as leaving a student teacher alone in charge), I would never have detected difficulties that Jim was having with certain aspects of instruction. Being dyslexic (a diagnosis not shared with me until I became aware of difficulties he was having with correcting papers and teaching spelling demons), we were able to work out techniques in preparation for both class instruction and assessments. In addition, Jim made some errors in grammatical instruction that required correction, so that students were not provided with misinformation.

2. Mentoring a student teacher—if done correctly—is a synergistic experience. While the student teacher observes the veteran, the cooperating teacher is forced to ask, "Who am I? What is my primary role? What am I doing in this class? And, why am I doing it this way?" These are intimidating questions for a veteran who has been going about his or her business with little evaluation—these questions are not for the faint of heart.

    Journal Reflection: The cooperating teacher must recognize that he or she is placing him- or herself under a microscope, and what he or she see may not always be attractive. From a positive standpoint, however, this means that veteran teachers can find themselves affirmed, enriched, and better educators from the lessons learned in this evaluative experience.

3. If a cooperating teacher sees as his or her mission the need to prepare future educators, he or she must be open and, if necessary, confrontational.

    Journal Reflection: That last word has a negative ring to it in a society made so sensitive to other's feelings that correcting errors may be regarded as a function of the past. If a cooperating teacher, however, observes something amiss, he or she has an obligation to correct it, or a disservice is being provided to both the student teacher and the many students who may be entrusted to his or her care in the future. Confrontation does not need to be mean-spirited—it can serve as a moment of collective enlightenment when true learning takes place. It can be done politely.

When Jim stopped providing me with lesson plans and was falling behind, however, I was not subtle. I asked directly, "Jim, what is going on in your life that has produced such a change? Although a detailed daily lesson plan may not be realistic when teaching a full course load, at least an outline of your plan is needed. May I anticipate a return to this policy tomorrow?" Jim responded affirmatively and apologized. He explained that he needed to reduce the number of hours he was working after school, realizing that he could not function full-time as a teacher (albeit as a student teacher) and work 20 hours per week, as he had done when he was a university student. Jim understood, for future reference, that teaching demands far more than 30 hours per week—a significant amount of preparation work is carried on at home. It is crucial that lessons be prepared in advance. Some spontaneity is always welcome, but the lack of a lesson plan only translates into disorganization, with students being cheated in the process.

4. Many teachers are control freaks and find it difficult to assume the role of facilitator. Nowhere is one's need to let go more evident than in the role of a cooperating teacher. Standing back and releasing to another is an exhausting experience—it taxes the very fiber of a person, like myself, who takes pride in being on top of all matters. If Jim did not do things the way I would, was he wrong? Were my ways better just because they were mine? Was his approach as valid? And, heaven forbid, perhaps even better? Could I learn from him?

Journal Reflection: I came to call this disposition "letting go and letting Jim." It was one of the most difficult tasks for me. Watching Jim teach and neither interfering nor interrupting was not easy. Some students in the class would actually turn to the rear of the room in search of me to rectify, clarify, or explicate a topic. If Jim called on me or there was an opportunity to correct an error or oversight in process, I would occasionally do so. I tried my best, however, to avoid this and to give Jim his own space to sink or swim—minor corrections would always be possible later through a conference.

Conclusion: I was thrilled to be invited to Jim's commencement exercises, and he has come back to visit me on a number of occasions. Mentoring Jim was a defining experience for me as I became reacquainted with my own motivations. Jim's youthful energy and enthusiasm were infectious—I was renewed in my commitment to the education profession as a result. When he read *A Midsummer Night's Dream* with my class, for example, his puerile levity made me remember a time when I identified far more vicariously with the maddening and wonderful course of true love. What a wonderful experience this had been. Exhausted, I was, nevertheless, more than willing to repeat it again.

2. The department chair as mentor

Sally was a first-year teacher. She had taken many English classes in college, as well as secondary-education preparatory courses. She was new to the school and to the profession, and was unsure of herself. Sally opened the school year with a short-story unit and had a few problems evoking her students' interest. How, she wondered, if they were challenged by Poe and Hawthorne's prose, would she be able to stimulate their interest in the poetry of Dickinson or Longfellow? How could she make poetry come alive?

Serving as Sally's department chair, I had invited her to visit my junior English class. As luck would have it, I was introducing a unit on poetry. Perhaps, she later related, insights could be gained from observing a veteran teacher. She sat in the rear of my classroom during her free period and observed the following:

1. I distributed the photocopy of a poem that I had written the previous evening. The students were impressed that their teacher had taken the time to write a poem for them, and that he had the ability to do so.

2. Students were asked to read the poem silently to themselves, split up into groups of four, and spend 10 minutes in an attempt to provide an interpretation.

3. At the end of 10 minutes, each student was asked to open his or her journal and summarize what their group had discussed, and what they believed was the thematic intent of the poem.

4. I followed this by asking for volunteers to read their interpretations and a brief, lively discussion ensued.

5. I proceeded to place six terms on the chalkboard. They were: metaphor, simile, symbolism, alliteration, rhyme, and rhythm. Students were asked to return to their groups once more, in order to either share definitions for the terms with which they were familiar and/or find the definitions in the glossary of their textbooks. After a brief time period, six students were asked to place the definitions that they had obtained on the chalkboard.

6. While these definitions were posted on the board, each group was asked to find an example of each term within the poem. After a few minutes, these examples were solicited and also posted on the board next to the definitions of the respective terms.

7. Students were then asked to listen attentively to brief pieces of music to determine which beat (rhythm) most closely resembled the cadence of the words in the poem (i.e., if they were to place these words to music, which one would they select and why?).

8. Finally, just prior to the conclusion of the class, I made a connection between my poem, that we had worked on for the period, and a poem in their textbook. Longfellow's poem contained the same elements with which we were now familiar. It was pointed out that the literary devices under examination were not poetic attributes of the past with no connection to the present—they transcended time and place. Now they were

asked to analyze Longfellow's poem for homework. These juniors were to locate examples of five of the six elements in Longfellow's poem, along with writing a summary of its thematic intent—we would discuss the rhythm of the poem the following day.

Sally dialogued with me after the class, and said that she was impressed. She had just observed a very active classroom, with students engaging in cooperative learning, articulating their interpretations of the poem, writing on the chalkboard, listening to music, and making all of the connections to Longfellow's work in the homework assigned. Here was a lesson plan that she desired to emulate.

Journal Reflection: The function and responsibilities of a department chair can vary, according to the specific school, or school system, within which one works. Some department chairs are no longer given the responsibility of formally observing the members of their department. For over 13 years, I collectively chaired both the English and interdisciplinary studies departments at my Grades 9–12 high school. In that capacity, it was my responsibility to formally observe scores of teachers, some in their first year of teaching and others who had been teaching far longer than I. How can one serve as a mentor while chairing a department?

I believe that one of my primary functions is to encourage, affirm, and evaluate the professional educators within my department. If their classrooms are open to me, then my classroom must be open to them. Through collegial visitations of each other's classes, I have attempted to tear down the barrier between the evaluator and evaluated. With a common goal in mind to educate, the sharing of ideas at departmental meetings becomes the order of the day. At each meeting, specific members of the department are invited to share what has been going on within their classes. Photocopies of rubrics, portfolio assessments, and pedagogical successes (as well as failures) are open fodder for discussion and discernment. If I have observed a class where an interesting approach has been used, then (with the approval of that educator) I compliment them and ask them to share it with others at the monthly meeting. It is heartwarming to see the look of professional glee on the face of one recognized for the value of what one is doing. Likewise, imagine my delight when members of my department observe my class and ask for copies of the lesson, so that they may utilize it in their classes.

Educators carry out a very public service but, often, in isolation from each other. Rarely does one English teacher know what is going on in the English class of a colleague next door. By opening my door to them, I attempt to make them more comfortable, both when I observe their class and when they observe each other. I have utilized the procedure of cross-observation—for example, one team (in this case, a pair) of teachers observes another pair, who in turn, observes them. I often visit with these pairs and make their insights part of my formal evaluation.

Conferences both before and after the visitation of a class are also helpful, where I invite teachers to have me observe an aspect of the class that is of concern to them. For example: "Am I calling on the boys more than the girls?" "Can you hear me from the rear of the classroom?" "Do I really have a serious personality conflict with Johnny Smith?"

Of course, the department chair is responsible for a specific content area. Questions about whether sophomores have been adequately prepared for the writing of a research paper must be addressed. There is no reason, however, why professional pedagogical development should not be part of a department chair's jurisdiction. If not, where else does it belong in schools in which schoolwide administrators are burdened with more and more responsibilities?

3. The teammate as mentor

Tom was my fourth teammate since I began teaching an innovative interdisciplinary course called Humanities some seven years earlier. Each one of my comrades was unique and their personalities were reflected in this integrated program that combines English, social studies, and fine arts in a double-period block each day. My previous two partners were first-year teachers, who remained with the program for brief periods of time before either moving onto other departments or leaving the school. I mentored both of them, since they were new to teaching, let alone to an interdisciplinary program. Tom, I thought, would be different. He was a veteran teacher, having taught in both public and private high schools for some 25 years. Although I was the department chair, I deferred all observations of this team-taught class to the vice principal of academics, since I could be neither an observer nor an evaluator of my own team.

Every seven days, Tom and I designated a common free period as a planning session. During this time, we planned the classes for the next week, plotted the assessments, and discussed the material to be covered, as well as the performance of the students. In addition, we examined our pedagogical approaches and reflected on successes and shortcomings. Tom would frequently ask me, "How would you evaluate my teaching this past week? Are you pleased with my performance?" I had indicated to Tom, at the start of the school year, that I wanted the two of us to be very open with each other—if anything I did, or did not do, bothered him, he was to tell me so directly. Likewise, I would do the same with him.

Tom was soon to add another dimension to our working partnership. Since he was new to the school and the program, he formally asked if I would be his mentor. He asked, and I readily accepted. As a result, I not only planned the double-period, interdisciplinary block with him, but I also assisted him in working with unfamiliar technology, entering grades, and answering a myriad of questions made possible by my 14 years on the scene, to which he had just arrived.

My assumption was that this would be a far easier year, since Tom was a veteran. Boy, was I wrong. Somehow—either because Tom had retired from public-school teaching eight years earlier, or because he had taught at a private junior high school before arriving at our senior high school—he erroneously thought that teaching involved the mere presentation of facts in his social studies component. With papers on a desk behind which he frequently sat, an uncomfortable somnolence descended upon the room when he took center stage. When

Tom finished, there I was, dramatically reenacting a scene while standing on a desk, moving between rows, filling the room with enthusiastic appreciation of the subject matter, and engaging the students in hands-on activities and cooperative learning. I did not want such a shocking contrast to continue and neither did Tom—students were beginning to take sides, and Tom was getting rightfully exasperated by the comparison. This was not a competition—I neither desired nor solicited the role of superior teacher. What was I to do?

At our next meeting, when Tom asked his question about reviewing his performance, I seized the opportunity to dialogue with him on the differences in our teaching styles. I indicated to him that no one style of instruction is better than another, but that ninth-grade students need to be actively engaged in the learning process—they cannot just sit there and listen. That was the primary reason why I taught the way that I did. There were two key challenges, however, to face, even after Tom's admission that he could feel the students' listlessness setting in during his instruction. Firstly, Tom did not know how to change his style, since it was an integral part of his character for so many years; secondly, he was uncomfortable in experimenting with new approaches. Both of these issues were interrelated to each other, and Tom and I embarked on a plan of action to address them.

Firstly, I indicated that Tom could not sit behind his desk—he could not establish such a physical barrier to the students in a class of 40 youngsters. Secondly, since this was a team-taught class with both of us in the classroom at the same time for both periods, Tom needed to know that, whatever he did, I was there for physical, moral, pedagogical, and cooperative support—if a plan failed, we both could pick up the pieces. Thirdly, several suggestions were derived cooperatively through our dialogue that would improve the class and make it more dynamic.

One proposal was that Tom present the new material to the students, rather than following a pattern of asking them questions about the reading they were to have done the night before (most of them were not doing the reading because it was difficult for them to comprehend it). A daily list of written or dictated questions for homework, based on what was discussed in class, was created. Students would come to realize that their homework, and the material covered in class, had a direct connection—by paying attention in class, they would have the answers to their homework questions readily available in their notes. I also suggested that Tom might want to include these same homework questions on the students' next test to allow for success, an element that was significantly lacking thus far. Tom added daily small quizzes on the material to encourage good listening and notetaking skills. I also suggested the use of an overhead projector, which Tom tried and learned to enjoy using.

I had observed that when Tom asked a question he did not look up from his notes and/or looked only to one side of the room, thereby ignoring students who had their hands up for several minutes. In addition, he *overtalked* the question (i.e., he continued to ask many aspects of the same question before calling on anyone), which discouraged students from taking a stab at the answer. Once aware of these idiosyncrasies, Tom looked up when he asked a question, made a point to wait for a reply without talking, and affirmed the students who had responded. Soon, more hands began to be raised, and students were more actively engaged.

Tom was willing to experiment with students working in small groups on map skills who would share the information uncovered later in a larger class setting. Board work and projects still did not come easily to Tom. He was trying, but he was ever hesitant to release traditional teacher control of the classroom.

Journal Reflection: This is a work-in-progress. Just because a teacher may be described as a veteran does not mean that they are enmeshed in the world of contemporary pedagogical techniques. On the contrary, the new ways, to many, are defective and inadequate. Tom had never been partnered with another teacher—he had not been in a position to ask another for constructive criticism of his teaching methods. To his credit, he was open and receptive to suggestions. Nevertheless, I frequently wonder how many Toms there may be out there in the world of education—veteran teachers never afforded the opportunity to be renewed and challenged by a mentor. Mentoring, for me, has taken on a totally new dimension with Tom. I hope that I can prove the adage wrong and succeed in teaching an old dog new tricks. It certainly will be interesting trying.

Conclusion

Still Learning

The famous English novelist, Aldous Huxley, died on the same day as John F. Kennedy's assassination, on November 22, 1963. In a newspaper article published after his death, Huxley is reported to have taken up painting 10 years earlier. He was pleased that one of his works was displayed at a local festival in Lancaster, and he remarked that, at a gallery a short distance from this site, hung a drawing for which the artist, Goya, had received no such recognition. The painting represents an old man walking with the aid of two sticks, and below the drawing Goya had written the words, *Aun aprendo*, which translates to mean "still learning."

> This image could rightfully suit all mentors, for "learning is the fundamental process and the primary purpose of mentoring" (Zachary, 2000, p. 1).

Mentors must love what he or she do, for it is out of this love that the desire to give freely and openly to others is born. However, sometimes the best of intentions get derailed by inadequate preparation of the relationship and/or the inability, on the part of the mentor or the mentee, to fully partake in what Zachary terms the "enabling phase" (Zachary, 2000, p. xvi). Although the less-than-successful examples stated earlier in this chapter may have been the result of personality quirks or inadequate teacher-education training, their explication is offered here not as a rationalization of failure, but rather to assist in the development of beneficial mentoring skills.

Unfortunately, while there was plenty of time and opportunity to thank each other and reflect on the successes, rarely did I, as mentor, pursue dialoguing with the "nonsuccesses" at the conclusion of a mentoring relationship. What could this have achieved? For one thing, it would have forced both of us to review what we hoped to accomplish at the outset, and how far we had come. Even though the results may have been different than anticipated or desired, the outcomes could have been objectively analyzed for the mutual benefit of both parties.

To its advantage and detriment, teaching is a passionate profession. Hence, when a mentor and mentee are about to part company under less-than-optimum conditions—the case with Jessica, Alice, and Caitlin—few prolong it with a discussion. Yet, it might be a refreshing adjunct to the mentoring concept for such a meeting to take place. After all, hasn't this approach gained momentum in the business world in the form of the exit interview? In all three cases, this would have proved to be an asset. So much of what I have learned in reflection may have been gained at the time, and possibly new insights acquired. *Aun aprendo—*still learning.

If a person closes his or her eyes and thinks back to those who have made a difference in their lives, the picture of mentors and the authentic meaning of the word becomes evident (Dortch, 2000, p. 6). Thomas Dortch provides the vivid example of when he and his friends spent many an hour in the neighborhood barbershop, where he was informally mentored by his elders (Dortch, 2000, pp. 3–4). Likewise, the very essence of teaching is a mentoring process. Students are watching every move of their mentors daily, who teach them as much by example as they do by instructional techniques. Teachers are constantly reaching out to the young men and women entrusted to their care as advisors, coaches, and moderators, mentoring them in all aspects of their lives. Naturally, these same mentors want to reach out to colleagues in their field to pass on their wisdom, their knowledge, and their expertise. And they are enriched by the experience.

It is the contention of this writer that mentoring is not limited to the formal duties of a department chair, a cooperating teacher, or a team leader, but it is an integral aspect of the daily life of the teacher when he or she steps out of the classroom and interacts with colleagues in the halls, the teacher's lounge, or at meetings. Learning is the primary objective of education; it must be the reciprocal goal, for both mentor and mentee, in every mentoring relationship. A love of teaching translates to a love of learning. As mentor, the learning can take on an even more challenging and captivating dimension.

References

Campbell, D. E., & Campbell, T. A. (2000). The mentoring relationship: Differing perceptions of benefits. *College Student Journal, 34*(4), 516–523.

Casey, J. D., & Mitchell, R. (1996). Small epiphanies: The discoveries of beginning teachers. *Baylor Educator, 21*(1), 14–25.

Checkley, K., & Kelly, L. (1999). Toward better teacher education: A conversation with Asa Hilliard. *Educational Leadership, 56*(8), 58–62.

Delgado, M. (1999). Lifesaving 101: How an experienced teacher can help a beginner. *Educational Leadership, 56*(8), 27–29.

Dennis, G. (1993). Mentoring. *Education research consumer guide.* Washington, DC: Office of Educational Research and Improvement (OERI), U.S. Department of Education. (OR 93-3059. ERIC ED/OERI 92-38)

Donne, J. (1989). Meditation 17. In J. Pfordresher, G. V. Veidemanis, & H. McDonnell (Eds.). *England in literature* (pp. 283–284). Glenview, IL: Scott Foresman.

Dortch, T. W. (2000). *The miracles of mentoring: The joy of investing in our future.* New York: Doubleday.

Glickman, C. D., Gordon, S. P., & Ross-Gordon, J. M. (1998*). Supervision of instruction: A developmental approach* (4th ed.). Boston: Allyn & Bacon.

Hole, S., & McEntee, G. H. (1999). Reflection is at the heart of practice. *Educational Leadership, 56*(8), 34–37.

Jacobs, H. H. (1989). Design options for an integrated curriculum. In H. H. Jacobs (Ed.), *Interdisciplinary curriculum: Design and implementation* (pp. 13–24). Alexandria, VA: Association for Supervision and Curriculum Development.

Johnson, H. R. (2001). First-year teachers: Teaching mentoring in education. *Journal of Instructional Psychology, 28*(1), 44–50.

McKenna, G. (1998). Mentor training: The key to effective staff development. *Principal, 77*(3), 47–49.

Rogers, D. L., & Babinski, L. (1999). Breaking through isolation with new teaching groups. *Educational Leadership, 56*(8), 38–40.

Rowley, J. B. (1999). The good mentor. *Educational Leadership, 56*(8), 20–22.

Sinetar, M. (1998). *The mentor's spirit: Life lessons on leadership and the art of encouragement.* New York: St. Martin's Press.

Tell, C. (1999). Renewing the profession of teaching: A conversation with John Goodlad. *Educational Leadership, 56*(8), 14–19.

Wasley, P. (1999). Teaching worth celebrating. *Educational Leadership, 56*(8), 8–13.

Wicks, R. J. (2000). *Sharing wisdom: The practical art of giving and receiving mentoring.* New York: Crossroad.

Young, C. Y., & Wright, J. V. (2001). Mentoring: The components for success. *Journal of Instructional Psychology, 28*(3), 202–206.

Zachary, L. (2000). *The mentor's guide: Facilitating effective learning relationships.* New York: Jossey-Bass.

For Consideration:

1. How does the John Donne quote "no man is an island" relate to the teaching profession?
2. How can one judge if a mentoring relationship is successful?
3. Comment upon the five mentoring roles.

Section II

Mentoring as a Way
to Create a Community
of Teachers and Learners

Chapter 2

Mentoring in a Professional Community: Voices from the Field

Nancy Hennessey

How does a regional high school district address the needs of new staff members and facilitate their membership in its professional community? The response seems fairly obvious: by creating an induction process that includes both new-teacher training and a mentoring program. In fact, over 30 states, including New Jersey, have mandated support programs with this purpose (Portner, 1998, p. 3). The need for such structures is clear and well documented. According to the National Commission on Teaching and America's Future (1996), up to one third of new teachers leave in the first three years. This is an alarming statistic, in light of reports that we will need 2 million teachers over the next 10 years, as the majority of educators in schools today are at, or nearing, retirement age. There is also increasing concern about the quality of teacher candidates. In Margaret Wang's (2000) words,

> Although some fear that there will be insufficient numbers of teachers in
> the next decade, the most serious problem may be the preparedness and
> quality of the present and prospective teaching force (p. 1).

Given the impending shortage of candidates, and the knowledge that what teachers know makes the difference in improved student learning (National Foundation for the Improvement of Education (NFIE), 1996), there is little doubt about the necessity of a support system focused on the attainment of professional competency.

However, there is a second, perhaps less obvious, response to this question; namely, by creating a supervision-evaluation system for all teachers that is committed to excellence in teaching and learning, and is based on rigorous standards and comprehensive, differentiated professional-growth opportunities. The induction system is an integral component of this system, and is a vehicle for ensuring competence and continuous professional growth. The district has, in fact, refined its system twice in the last six years and, each time, considered how mentoring would, and should, play an effective role in the supervision of new teachers. Dr. Thomas McGreal, who worked with us on a redesign of our supervision-evaluation system, reminded us that each school's culture is different, and that all new staff need opportunity to learn about district and school norms, practices and procedures, and to become members of the community. Hence, a unique feature of our program is that we mentor new, experienced teachers as well as inexperienced ones. The third response to meeting the needs of the novice teacher is embedded within the philosophy and the culture of the district that created the supervision-evaluation system described above. It is, in fact, the belief that an ongoing, collaborative process is the most meaningful vehicle for creating and implementing effective programs. It reflects an acknowledgement that educators are indeed the "greatest untapped resource" in our schools. By providing an opportunity for their voices to be heard and for them to work together, we value them as professionals and validate their membership in a professional learning community. Karen Seashore Louis, Helen Marks, & Sharon Kruse (1996) have identified five elements of professional community, such as:

- shared norms and values
- collective focus on student learning
- collaboration
- deprivatized practice
- reflective dialogues

For the West Morris Regional High School District, a commitment to professional community has been instrumental in providing a framework for collaboration, as evidenced in our design process and ongoing evaluation of our mentoring program, as well as other initiatives. At this point, some explanation of how the concept of professional community translates into district practices would be informative. A literature review yields several descriptors of such communities that are identifiable in our culture, including: (1) opportunity to discuss ideas and perspectives collectively; (2) development of shared norms and values; and (3) a willingness to be collectively responsible for initiatives that ultimately lead to excellence in teaching and learning. Additionally, staff development is valued, differentiated opportunities for growth is provided, and there is a norm of continuous growth and contribution. As a result of a collaborative workplace that encourages communication and nurtures productive group work, diverse voices have had the opportunity to contribute to, and shape, our mentoring program.

Several states have well-defined, elaborate mentoring systems that serve as models, i.e., the California Beginning Teacher Model. At the time of the initial development of our system, New Jersey provided only a basic framework that outlined roles and responsibilities, leaving program specifics to the local school district. Of note is the fact that the statutory requirements for mentoring novice teachers have been recently revised and are more comprehensive in nature. However, the district recognized a mentoring system as an immediate need in 1997, and viewed the lack of guidance as a welcome opportunity for our "voices" to create an implementation and evaluation design that reflected best practice, and that aligned with our district mission and goals and perhaps, most importantly, matched our context—that of a regional high school district.

Who, then, are the voices that contributed to an ever-evolving program, and how did the district capture their collective thinking? Frankly, our vision initially focused on administrators and mentors, but it soon became apparent, as we engaged in the process, that it indeed "takes a whole village" to realize the potential of mentoring. The National Foundation for the Improvement of Education (1996) suggests that an effective mentor is an essential participant in the process but should not be held solely responsible for the induction of new teachers. This obligation must be shared more broadly by the entire faculty and administration. Hal Pornter (2001, pp. 47–52) speaks to the specific roles that administrators, nonmentoring veteran teachers, mentors, new teachers, and a mentoring coordinator can assume. Over the course of the last five years, it is, in fact, all of these voices that have contributed to the West Morris Regional High School District program, as it exists today. To understand how, and what role they have played, it is necessary to review the phases of development and implementation.

In 1997, we recognized, for various reasons, that the informal program in place, while well intentioned, lacked direction and substance. Almost simultaneously, the district was the recipient of a Goals 2000 grant that provided resources for addressing these concerns and allowed us to invite interested staff members to participate as members of a newly formed "Mentoring Team." These voices were instrumental in creating the district's first formal model, including written guidelines for the mentoring process. Their work was the result of training, research, and many hours of discussion that led to a definition of purpose, goals, mentor qualifications, mentor selection, roles and responsibilities, and program evaluation. This team, comprised of one administrator and 14 teachers, committed to ongoing involvement in the program. Over the last five years, they have served as mentors, facilitators of training, and program evaluators. All of them, who are still teaching in the district, contributed to, and/or participated in, the "Mentoring Revisited" meeting held last year. They revisited and updated the district guidelines (see insert-contents). Additionally, they brought the voices of new and veteran teachers and administrators (captured through ongoing discussions and surveys) into the room. The team upgraded the district's purpose statement to read:

> The purpose of mentoring is to provide a supportive learning environment, in which experienced and inexperienced new teachers understand, and gain confidence in, instructional competencies, increase professional knowledge, and become contributing members of the professional community.

Additionally, they asserted that a mentoring program is most successful when it:

- reflects specific culture and beliefs;
- is built upon a broad base of commitment and participation;
- is designed, implemented, managed, assessed, and nurtured; and
- receives ongoing support and resources.

The district's goals are based on assumptions that Lipton & Wellman (2001, p. x–xi) identify as being central to collaborative learning-focused relationships, such as:

- Mentoring relationships offer the opportunity for reciprocal growth and learning.
- Induction is an investment in retention, integration, and continual growth.
- A central goal for the mentoring program is improved student learning.

Of note is the fact that one of the team's primary goals called for creating a climate of collegiality, thus creating the means for listening to the "voices" of our new staff members. They also articulated that the expected results of a successful mentoring program should be the successful integration of new teachers into the school community, increased instructional competency, a commitment to professional growth, a cooperative work environment, and increased retention of teachers.

It is not surprising, in a district committed to professional community, that building a cadre of trained mentors, who have the capacity to serve, was recognized as essential to the success of the program. While the mentor-selection process aligns with New Jersey code, the mentoring team also created the West Morris Regional High School District definition of mentoring and outlined characteristics of effective mentors. The guidelines state that:

Mentors Provide:
- positive feedback;
- anticipate and address the needs of new teachers;
- share experiences and suggestions;
- build confidence;
- challenge to higher levels;
- unconditional support; and
- serve as role models and model best practice.

Mentors Have:
- high expectations for themselves and the profession;
- successful working and teaching experiences with adults;
- excellent communication skills;
- a wide variety of instructional skills and knowledge of the curriculum;
- an understanding of learning theories, human growth and development, principles of evaluation, student evaluation, and diversity of students' backgrounds;
- an ability to deal with conflict;
- high integrity; and
- an ability to offer unconditional support to new teachers.

Team members also recommended that new teachers be assigned mentors from the same discipline and, when possible, teach the same courses. In a high school setting, this is particularly critical because of the focus on deep-content knowledge, as well as pedagogy. In fact, with few exceptions, this is what happens.

The team also acknowledged the necessity of specific training and support systems for new teachers and mentors. They have been continually involved in upgrading the preparation process for mentors. Three members of the team and me have designed and delivered training for both mentors and new teachers for the last five years. As of now, mentors participate in an introductory, full-day session prior to the start of school. They learn about:

- purposes of mentoring;
- skills, qualities, and abilities of mentoring;
- needs of mentors;
- needs of new teachers;
- mentor roles and responsibilities;
- support strategies; and
- benefits of mentoring.

Members of the team have also identified the need for the initial training session for new teachers and mentors to be scheduled simultaneously, so that they can participate in a shared session focused on a common language and understanding of district expectations, teaching standards, and the professional development portfolio required of all nontenured teachers. Recognizing the importance of peer observation and coaching, the team continually voiced the need for training in this area. As a result, additional sessions have been scheduled during the school year that address the purpose, components, and essential skills of peer coaching. The team has also been instrumental in advocating for continued support for mentors through share sessions, provision of resources, and additional training opportunities. They have advocated for shared planning periods and proximity to facilitate communication, knowing that these conditions are often difficult to attain, whether in an elementary, middle, or high school setting, but are also very important.

Virtually every member of the mentoring team has served as a mentor to a new teacher. As a result, they have been able to consistently bring their voices to the critical topic of roles and responsibilities. Their original design called for meeting regularly to discuss policies and procedures, planning, delivery, and assessing of instruction, as well as specific student-related concerns. Mentors also were expected to visit new teacher's classrooms, using a peer-coaching model to provide nonevaluative feedback. These expectations have been continually upgraded by the team. In a learning community, all staff members are involved in the design and implementation of initiatives that connect to school and district goals. They are cognizant of the mission of the school and how important it is that all members be involved. These other voices influenced the process by reminding the team of what new teachers need to know about the culture. Consequently, the team has upgraded original activities by suggesting potential topics for discussion that are germane to our context (i.e., Long Range Plan initiatives and the role of teachers as leaders in the district). All of the new teachers in the district also participate in a professional development portfolio process (inquiry-based). The mentoring team recommended that the focus be on the creation of the Planning Binder (a district innovation and requirement), and that mentors work directly with new teachers in overseeing development. In fact, mentors join their new teachers on the initial day of training to discuss the planning-binder requirements and continue the discussion throughout the school year. Of significance is the growing recognition that all new teachers are indeed at different stages of development and, hence, mentors may need to focus on different topics more specific to teacher needs. The team has begun the work of identifying differentiated needs of new, inexperienced (provisional and alternate route) and new, experienced teachers. A sample of this endeavor follows.

Alternate Route:
- knowledge of child development (research-based)
- adjustment to deep-content knowledge base to student levels of ability
- "deconstruction" of curriculum concepts into manageable components
- knowledge of basic act of teaching (methodology/assessment)
- setting long-term curriculum goals and pacing
- understanding of community and how to interact effectively
- time management (professional versus personal lives)

Provisional Teacher
- establishment of "self" in the classroom (conveying a presence)
- translation of theory into practice
- time management (professional versus personal lives)
- movement beyond "basic" knowledge of content or subject area
- emotional support and nurturance
- knowledge of culture

Experienced Teacher
- knowledge of climate and culture
- assistance in understanding expectations
- support in rethinking and adjusting to change
- knowledge of department, goals, and curriculum expectations

Yet another set of voices, that has been particularly instrumental in the evolution of the district program, is that of the mentors and new teachers. Their collective experiences are gathered through needs assessment, informal and structured discussions, and written feedback. New teachers and mentors respond to questionnaires about their needs at the beginning of the year. We ask new teachers to share their responses with their mentors, to begin the dialogue around needed supports. Luncheon meetings throughout the school year provide the opportunity for professional conversations about what has worked, what is next, what is on their minds, and what to do and when. In this way, we are able, administratively, to continually assess what supports and resources new teachers and mentors need at any given moment in time. We've also learned the value of both shared and separate meetings that allow for an exchange of information specific to each group's issues and concerns. Early in the school year, mentors have an opportunity to talk with one another about the activities they have engaged in, and to identify each other as resources for problems they have encountered. For example, during a recent meeting, mentors were able to offer assistance to one of their colleagues in the area of assessment, specifically in the development of rubrics. While all mentors are experienced, proficient teachers, their levels of expertise differ, and the opportunity for supporting each other is critical. Similar opportunities for new teachers are provided, and they have consistently identified the need for more information at different times of the year. For example, mid-year concerns that surface are:

- procedures for incomplete grades;
- mid-term protocols and responsibilities; and
- student placement at differentiated course levels.

The voices of our new teachers and mentors also play an important role in both a formative and summative evaluation of our mentoring program. Throughout the year, we gather data through open-ended, informal, and structured conversations, interviews, and, most importantly, through an end-of-year survey. Mentors respond to a series of questions that profile activities, resources used, and supports that facilitated their task. Additionally, they articulate challenges and benefits. Mentors tell us that they value the district guidelines, written information on mentoring, training, and network meetings as sources of information for understanding their roles and responsibilities. They advise their successors not to assume what their protégés need. One valuable source of information for mentors is a needs assessment that new teachers complete and are encouraged to share as a focal point for discussion. Equally valuable suggestions offered include helping even when it's not solicited and rejecting the idea that their mentee should be a "clone" of themselves. They indicate that experienced and inexperienced teachers need encouragement, enculturation, and opportunities for sharing and reflection. The primary difference, of course, surfaces in the areas of content and pedagogy, so discussion topics and peer-coaching focus differ in terms of depth. Our mentors also provide the rationale for engaging in this process. Those who have been involved in mentoring programs can attest that participation often results in a professional transformation for the experienced teacher. Joellen Killion (1990) studied the benefits for experienced teachers and reported that:

> adults in mid- to late-career, typically in the 35–50 age bracket, have the need to find meaningful ways to feel valued, make a significant commitment to the next generation, and share their accumulated experiences. They also feel a need for personal renewal and revival (p. 33).

Our mentors tell us that the process prompts them to reexamine their practice, update professional strategies based on insights, and leads to further understanding of the complexity of teaching and learning. On an individual level, mentors reported that they have made new friends, learned how to help someone "shine," and reveled in watching the growth of their colleague. Time remains the greatest challenge—and, to a lesser degree, in our context, the differing needs of the alternate-route teacher. Mentors' responses also provide direction for the future, such as an increased focus on peer coaching.

Similarly, new teachers profile experiences and respond to prompts about learning and additional needs. Not surprisingly, their responses support and, in some instances, extend their mentors' ideas. What is highly evident from their comments is the importance of having a mentor who celebrates accomplishments, provides positive constructive feedback, takes time to talk regularly, shares resources, and "listens, listens, listens," with empathy. District mentors can take pride in the fact that new teachers indicate that their needs are fulfilled and, most importantly, they feel they have "someone to go to with questions (silly or not), or to talk to when feeling a 'bit down.'" Inherent in mentoring is both teaching and learning. Some lessons learned included organization, setting high standards for student performance, working with parents and peers, instructional design, and assessment strategies. One new teacher's response to the question about important learning gained from his or her mentor was, "Students are the most important thing in my job." The new teachers have also given us direction on how to refine both new teacher and mentor programs. The challenges they identified are common to most new teachers, such as classroom and time management, discipline, planning, curriculum, and adapting to the school's culture. Of note are their comments on understanding and fulfilling expectations of the planning binder, as required by the portfolio process, and working with difficult students. There is a common thread among their responses that reinforces the need to attend to emotional and psychological support that goes beyond policies, practices, and procedures.

Mentor and teacher voices continually remind us that trust and respect are the cornerstones of a professional-learning community. Knowing that these factors are key to successful mentoring, we ask mentors and new teachers how they build collegial relationships with mentees. They stress the importance of open, honest communication, confidentiality, and acceptance. Their responses convey their ability to view the beginning teacher as a developing person and professional. James Rowley (1999) tells us that "accepting mentors do not judge or reject mentees as poorly prepared, overconfident, naive, or defensive" (p. 20). Our mentors are able to identify strengths, and to see weaknesses as "challenges." It is critical that we, as a district, continue to revisit and reinforce the concept that there is a difference between mentoring and evaluation; namely, using a collegial versus hierarchical approach, collecting data for reflection rather than for judgment, and the confidential nature of their mentor-mentee relationship. We have worked at respecting the confidential nature of the mentor–new teacher relationship and continue to do so. When information is shared with administrators, it is used to support the individual involved, so that they can meet expectations. Similarly, administrators sometimes share concerns and/or areas of need observed, so that mentors can work with new teachers in a meaningful manner. The real difficulty lies not in articulating the difference between mentoring and evaluation but in achieving a level of understanding in all involved (the rest of the village), so that everyone's actions convey this belief. For the last two years, our new teachers and mentors have responded to a series of questions directly related to their experiences. Overall, mentor and new teacher feedback has been both a source of validation of our efforts and a direction for improvement.

Another voice, namely my own, has also contributed to the shaping of our system for new staff. At the same time, I have assumed the role of MOM (mentor of mentors). Portner (2001) describes this person as someone who is available to mentors and accountable to the team. This person:

- thoroughly understands everyone's roles and responsibilities;
- is clear about the purpose and goals of the program;
- is familiar with the context (school and district); and
- has the authority and resources to do the job.

In essence, I have been the chief advocate, along with the building principals, for what is a critical process in any school setting. Like many other administrators who are called upon for leadership in this area, I have worked at creating the structure and process, allocating the resources, and identifying the participants. While this is a critical role, it is the collaborative work of the mentor team, mentors and new teachers that has resulted in its effective design and implementation. It is the mentors and new teachers who do "a mentoring commercial" each year at a faculty meeting, encouraging their colleagues to participate in the process. They do this by telling their story—new teacher and mentor together. It is a story that conveys the importance and benefit to the school community and to the individual.

Our collective actions, as we engage in the process and the practice connected to this program, are not only representative of the common elements of professional community identified earlier but embody the essence of them. Our challenge is to sustain our ability to create opportunities to listen to the voices involved in district initiatives. Our pride in our commitment to professional community is appropriate, since we know that the end result of collaborative workplaces is a collective sense of responsibility for making a difference in students' lives. We have reason to celebrate!

References

Killion, J. (1990). The benefits of an induction program for experienced teachers. *Journal of Staff Development, 11*(4), 32–36.

Lipton, L., & Wellman, B. (2001). *Mentoring matters: Practical guide to learning focused relationships.* Sherman, CT: MiraVia LLC.

Louis, K. S., Marks, H. M., & Kruse, S. (1996). Teachers' professional community in restructuring schools. *American Educational Research Journal, 33*(4) 757–798.

National Commission on Teaching and America's Future. (1996). *What matters most: Teaching for America's future.* New York: National Commission on Teaching and America's Future.

National Foundation for the Improvement of Education (NFIE). (1996). Teachers take charge of their learning: Transforming professional development for student success. Washington, DC: The National Education Association (NEA) Foundation.

Portner, H. (1998). *Mentoring new teachers.* Thousand Oaks, CA: Corwin Press.

Portner, H. (2001). *Training mentors is not enough.* Thousand Oaks, CA: Corwin Press.

Rowley, J. (1999). The good mentor. *Educational Leadership, 56*(8), 20–22.

Wang, M. (2000). New teachers for a new century: Recommendations from a national invitational conference. *The CEIC Review, 9*(1), 1.

ADDENDUM

West Morris Regional High School District Mentoring Program

The purpose of mentoring is to provide a supportive, learning environment, in which experienced and inexperienced new teachers understand, and gain confidence in, instructional competencies, increase professional knowledge, and become contributing members of the professional community.

A mentoring program is most successful when it:
- reflects specific culture and beliefs;
- is built upon a broad base of commitment and participation;
- is designed, implemented, managed, assessed, and nurtured; and
- receives ongoing support and resources.

The results of a mentoring program should be the successful integration of new teachers into the school community, increased instructional competency, a commitment to professional growth, a cooperative work environment, and increased retention of teachers.

The West Morris Regional High School District's Mentoring Program is based upon the assumption that new teachers are "well-prepared in content and theory" but still have much to learn about putting their knowledge to work.

The goals of the West Morris Regional High School District's Mentoring Program are to:
- identify exemplary teaching skills and practices necessary to acquire and maintain excellence in teaching—through observation, conversation, planning, and practicing;
- develop the professional knowledge and attitudes that are vital to success throughout a teacher's career—professional development within the district, working closely with a context expert in your discipline, reading, and research;
- enhance a teacher's knowledge of, and the strategies related to, Core Curriculum Standards—discussion with discipline peers;
- reduce the concerns and assist new teachers in adjusting to the challenges common to teaching (e.g., discipline, classroom management, interaction with parents, diversity in students, and instructional issues);
- integrate new teachers into the culture of the school, the district, and the community;
- provide opportunities for new and experienced teachers to analyze, and reflect upon, their teaching and build a foundation for the continued study of teaching—opportunity to learn from each other;

- instill a climate for collegiality and experimentation—develop relationship based on trust and give-and-take; and
- retain highly qualified new and experienced teachers.

Mentors Defined

- Knowledgeable
- Available
- Caring
- Supportive
- Enthusiastic
- Trustworthy
- Intuitive

- Risk-takers
- Explorers
- Guides
- Listeners
- Advisors
- Friends
- Coaches

Mentors Provide:
- positive feedback;
- anticipate and address the needs of new teachers;
- share experiences and suggestions;
- build confidence;
- challenge to higher levels;
- unconditional support; and
- serve as role models and model best practice.

Mentors Have:
- high expectations for themselves and the profession;
- successful working and teaching experiences with adults;
- excellent communication skills;
- a wide variety of instructional skills and knowledge of the curriculum;
- an understanding of learning theories, human growth and development, principles of evaluation, student evaluation, and diversity of students' backgrounds;
- an ability to deal with conflict;
- high integrity; and
- an ability to offer unconditional support to new teachers.

Mentor Selection

It is recommended that a *cadre of mentors, representing each discipline, be created.* The cadre should consist of those individuals who comprise the mentoring team and staff members who have participated in formal training to date. Additional members of this cadre will be identified through a process that includes:
- completion of an application form
- submission of three letters of recommendation

A team comprised of administrators and mentors will oversee this process and recommend mentors.

To be considered as a candidate, applicants should be:
- New Jersey–certified in subject area and/or professional area to which the new teacher is assigned;
- tenured and currently teaching in the district or have three years experience and currently teaching in the district;
- committed to the goals of the West Morris Regional High School District;
- knowledgeable of both discipline-specific content and pedagogy;
- knowledgeable of the culture and expectations of the school, district, and community;
- knowledgeable of the district's long-range goals, objectives, strategies, and the resources committed to this effort; and
- willing to participate in required training and meetings.

Additionally, the following criteria will be considered in the selection process:
- peer-coaching experience
- demonstrated commitment to professional development

Mentor-Mentee Responsibilities

- Both mentor and mentee function as a team.
- Mentor functions as a member of the support team (comprised of mentor, a building administrator, and director of staff development).
- Both participate in district training meetings and mentor-mentee meetings.
- Both contribute to a compatible working relationship.
- Both work to assess the background of the new teacher and determine the type, and amount, of support needed.
- Mentor orients the new teacher to the district and school policies, procedures, and expectations.
- Mentee is encouraged to seek answers to questions and concerns.
- Mentor visits the new teacher's classroom once per marking period and provides feedback, coaching, and support.
- Mentee visits mentor's, or other same discipline teacher's, classroom once per marking period to observe effective teaching practice.
- Both are responsible for recording and maintaining observation record logs.
- Mentor orients the new teacher to discipline-specific curriculum.
- Mentee is responsible for following curriculum content.
- Mentor models effective teaching techniques.
- Mentee demonstrates effective teaching techniques.
- Both are available for informal consultation.
- Mentor assists the new teacher in the development of a planning binder.
- Mentee is responsible for sharing and discussing the contents of the planning binder.

Note:
1. All observations and feedback provided by the mentor are for the purpose of professional development and support, and should be considered confidential.
2. Mentors may share responsibility for a first-year teacher with one or more other mentor teachers.

Potential Topics for Discussion and Activities

Suggested topics and activities that mentors should consider addressing with new teachers:

Teaching Environment:
Collection of information about students, school, district, and community
*   explanation of chain of command
*   discussion of community expectations
*   provision of policies
*   preparation for "Back To School Night"
*   review of district Long Range Plan
*   explanation of attendance procedures
*   discussion of discipline policies

Learning Environment:
Establishment of climate
*   review of discipline policies and procedures
*   discussion of needs of special-education students
*   development of classroom rules
*   review of conference procedures
*   explanation of the role of teachers as leaders in the district

Student Assessment:
Development and analysis of student product
*   development and sharing of discipline-specific rubrics
*   review of samples of graded assessments
*   sharing of assessment tools
*   modeling of grading procedures
*   discussion of differentiated grading
*   completion of interim reports and comments
*   development of mid-term and finals

Planning and Preparation:
Development of planning and preparation
*   development of Planning Binder
*   development of daily and unit plans

- preparation for observation—pre- and postconferencing
- samples of lesson plans
- review of monthly calendar
- differentiation of lessons between levels

Instructional Experiences:
Explanation of effective strategies and activities
- discussion of technology applications
- modeling and discussion of effective strategies
- discussion of development of individual style and adjustment to student needs
- sharing of effective activities

Professional Growth:
Development of professional growth plans and participation in growth activities
- sharing of professional development opportunities within discipline
- discussion of options available for growth
- sharing of own professional growth focus
- development of Planning Binder

Analysis of Practice:
Use of observation and coaching
- refinement of practice as it relates to descriptors of effective teaching

Differentiated Activities

In addition to the generic responsibilities of the mentor teacher, the mentoring team has identified differentiated needs for the following.

Alternate Route:
- knowledge of child development (research-based)
- adjustment to deep-content knowledge base to student levels of ability
- "deconstruction" of curriculum concepts into manageable components
- knowledge of basic act of teaching (methodology/assessment)
- setting long-term curriculum goals and pacing
- understanding of community and how to interact effectively
- time management (professional versus personal lives)

Provisional Teacher:
- establishment of "self" in the classroom (conveying a presence)
- translation of theory into practice
- time management (professional versus personal lives)
- movement beyond "basic" knowledge of content or subject area

- emotional support and nurturance
- knowledge of culture

Experienced Teacher:
- knowledge of climate and culture
- assistance in understanding expectations
- support in rethinking and adjusting to change
- knowledge of department, goals, and curriculum expectations

Mentor Training and Meetings

All mentors are required to participate in an introductory, full-day training session at the beginning of the school year.

The focus of the initial training session is the development of knowledge and skills considered to be critical to an effective mentoring program. Participants will learn about:
- purposes of mentoring;
- skills, qualities and abilities of mentoring;
- needs of mentors;
- needs of new teachers;
- mentor roles and responsibilities;
- support strategies; and
- benefits of mentoring.

A second full-day training session will be conducted at a time to be determined each year. The focus of this session will be the development of peer-coaching skills.

Follow-up meetings will be held throughout the school year to address topics and issues specific to mentor–new teacher needs.

Support for mentors will be provided through:
- share sessions with the mentor coordinator;
- training opportunities; and
- resource materials.

Mentor-New Teacher Activities

An initial meeting between the mentor and the new teacher should be held prior to the beginning of school, to provide an opportunity for introductions and a sharing of expectations.

Mentors are expected to meet regularly with first-year teachers (weekly) and new, experienced teachers (biweekly) to discuss policies and procedures, planning and preparation, and curriculum and assessment issues, as well as specific problems and/or concerns.

Mentors should also visit new teachers' classrooms, using a peer-observation/coaching model, to provide nonevaluative feedback, and to share ideas (once per marking period). New teachers should visit the mentor's classroom to observe effective teaching practice (once per marking period).

Mentors and new experienced teachers may adjust recommended visitation times.

Mentors and new teachers will meet three to four times during the school year with the staff developer to:

- share effective practices;
- participate in the development of the Planning Binder;
- assess needs and share support strategies; and
- evaluate and provide feedback on mentoring program.

Program Evaluation

The systematic collection of information regarding activities, characteristics, and outcomes of the program is essential to the success of a program. It is recommended that both formative and summative evaluation be used to provide a comprehensive scope of the effectiveness of the West Morris Regional High School District program.

The purpose of this evaluation will be:

- accountability; and
- program improvement.

The data shall include:

- program impact on job satisfaction;
- adequacy of time and training; and
- recommended program changes and additions.

The target audience will be:

- mentors;
- new teachers; and
- administration.

The annual method/means will include:

- informal/structured discussions; • mentor and new teacher;
- open-ended interviews; • mentor and new teacher;
- questionnaires (see appendix); • mentor and new teacher; and
- mentor program design meeting; • mentoring team.

Data will be collected at:

- mentor–new teacher meetings;
- mentor training; and
- mentor redesign meeting.

Results of this evaluation will be used to:
- identify strengths and weaknesses;
- implement program changes; and
- allocate needed resources.

Additional Recommendations for Effective Implementation

In reviewing effective mentoring programs and considering collective experiences, the mentoring team recommends that the following topics be addressed as the program evolves:

Scheduled Time:
- Common Planning
- Classroom Visitations
- Coaching Experiences

Proximity:
- Mentors and new teachers share classrooms.
- Mentors and new teachers' classrooms are located in the same general area.

Curriculum:
- Creation of a notebook of "model lessons" in specific subject areas.

Supervision/Evaluation:
- Mentors' roles are nonevaluative, and confidentiality and trust are critical to their relationship with new teachers. Administrators and mentors must be aware of the fine line between evaluation and supervision as they communicate about new teachers.

Mentoring Commercial

Mendham HS

Thanks for your willingness to participate in a "Mentoring Commercial." Next year, we will need approximately 22 mentors across the district.

We have a brief opportunity (10 minutes) at the faculty meeting on June 6th, in each building, to ask staff members to consider becoming a mentor.

Describe the mentoring program guidelines and training. ____, _____, and ____ will discuss the benefits of mentoring from the perspective of an experienced, first-year and alternate-route teacher.

Since our time is limited, we will use the following guidelines:

Description: 2 minutes

Benefits: 2 minutes
                     2 minutes
                     2 minutes

Q & A: 2 minutes

Mentor Reference Form

I believe that:

Applicant _____

School _____

possesses the requisite skills, knowledge, and attitude to effectively serve as a mentor for a new, inexperienced, or experienced teacher.

_____

Name

Mentor Application Form

Please return to _____ by _____

_____ I am interested in mentoring a new teacher for 200_–200_.

_____ I would like to be considered in the future.

_____

Name

<<mentfirst>> <<mentlast>>
West Morris HS

Dear <<mentfirst>>,

The district is most appreciative that you are willing to serve as a mentor for <firstname> <lastname> during the school year. The mentoring program is a critical component of our new teacher-support system.

As you know, training is required for all mentors. We have scheduled a full-day session for August in the West Morris Mendham Library from 8:30 a.m.– 3:00 p.m. The morning session for new mentors will focus on mentoring basics. Experienced mentors (who have participated in prior training) should plan on joining us at 11:30 a.m. for lunch and the afternoon session. At that time, we will address responsibilities related to the Descriptors of Effective Teaching.

New teachers will also be meeting that day. There will be an opportunity to get acquainted during morning coffee or lunch (provided by the district). I would suggest that you call your *mentee* prior to this date. <firstname>'s phone number is <phone>.

New teachers have been asked to complete the enclosed needs assessment. This could be used as a starting point for discussion at this time or on the meeting date. You will be approved at a board meeting this summer. Mentors for inexperienced teachers receive a yearly honorarium of $1,000, and mentors for experienced teachers receive $500. If you share this responsibility with a colleague, then the honorarium is divided equally. Thank you again for your professionalism. If you have any questions, please call me.

Sincerely,

Dear   ,

We are pleased that you will be joining the faculty of West Morris Mendham HS in September 2001. The district has designed a new teacher training program that addresses the competencies which are expected of all teachers. The initial training session, which is required for inexperienced and experienced teachers, will be held on <date> in the West Morris Mendham Library, from 8:30 a.m.– 3:00 p.m.

The district's mentoring program focuses on providing a supportive learning environment, in which new teachers, both experienced and inexperienced, can gain confidence in instructional competencies and/or increase professional knowledge. Your mentor will be <mentor>. Mentors will also be involved in training that day, and there will be an opportunity to become acquainted over morning coffee and lunch (provided by the district), and to address district expectations with your mentor during the afternoon. We have asked your mentor to contact you prior to this date. Please complete and bring the attached needs assessment so that it can be used to facilitate discussion. Should you have any questions, please contact me.

Sincerely,

For Consideration

1. Select one of the five elements of a professional community and explain why you feel it is the most important.
2. Select one of the elements that make a mentoring program most successful and explain why you feel it is important.
3. What topic(s) do you consider essential to include in a mentoring training day?
4. Explain how one specific strategy mentioned in this selection proves and reinforces the contention of the first chapter's author—". . . that mentoring is not limited to the formal duties of a department chair, cooperating teacher, or team leader, but it is an integral aspect of the daily life of the teacher . . ."

Chapter 3

The Importance of Being Mentored: A Convergence of Two Perspectives

Maribeth Edmunds

Introduction

Mentoring novice teachers has received widespread attention in public schools throughout the country—and for good reason. Teachers are leaving our classrooms at alarming rates, and those teachers with fewer than five years of experience represent the most dramatic increase in attrition. In 1990, approximately 1,500 novice teachers in my home state of New Jersey left the profession. By 1999, this number had risen to almost 3,000 (Wollmer, 2001). This trend, which plagues many states, when coupled with the growing number of veteran teachers preparing to retire, underscores a disturbing prediction—finding highly qualified teachers and retaining them will be more difficult than ever. One important way to do this is by providing novice teachers with skillful, nurturing, and reflective mentors.

Effective September 2001, New Jersey legislated a revised code to ensure "a teaching force that is highly skilled, well trained, and prepared to face the host of extraordinary challenges that the classroom will bring to the new Millennium." The Code asks for a "rigorous two-year mentoring program for all novice teachers that will provide confidential and ongoing support from experienced teachers." To do so, New Jersey awarded grants to 15 public school districts for the express purpose of piloting two-year mentoring programs. South Brunswick was among them.

As the mentor coordinator for the South Brunswick Public School District, it was my responsibility to design a new mentoring program for first- and second-year teachers. Also, I offered to mentor a novice teacher to gain a firsthand perspective of the relationship. From these two vantage points, I hoped to gain a clearer understanding of the importance of being mentored. By the end of the year, I had learned far more than I expected.

To prepare for over 250 faculty members, I conducted an in-depth review of the literature. From this work, the elements for the yearlong training program emerged.

Program Elements: "Preparing Reflective Mentors"

Theoretical Strand

South Brunswick's pilot, entitled *Preparing Reflective Mentors*, consists of three strands. The first is a theoretical foundation that forms the framework of the program. The fundamental concept is that induction into the teaching profession is not simply an event. Instead, it is a complex process that evolves over time, a process of "creating and inventing one's self-image as a teacher." Therefore, the Emerging Theory of Induction was introduced and described to the mentors (DeBolt, 1992). The next element of the theoretical strand involves Teacher Stages of Concerns Theory (DeBolt, 1992). All novice teachers experience: (1) the Survival Stage; (2) the Teaching Situation Stage; and (3) the Student Concern or Mastery Stage. The last theory used in this strand is based on Anderson & Shannon's seminal article, *Toward a Conceptualization of Mentoring* (1988). They identified five critical activities: teaching, sponsoring, encouraging, counseling, and befriending.

From this research on teacher induction, the overarching principles, objectives, and functions of the mentor were formulated for the 2000–2001 pilot year.

South Brunswick's Definition of Mentoring

Mentoring is a nurturing process, in which a more skilled, or experienced, teacher oversees the development of a novice for the purpose of improving his or her professional experience. To be successful, the mentor-novice relationship must be professional, caring, and confidential.

Observation-Coaching Strand

The second strand involves a formal mentor-coaching model, researched and designed by Claire Brusseau, South Brunswick's staff developer. Throughout the district, over 200 professional staff began visiting one another's classrooms for the purpose of collecting and reviewing objective data. Such a large-scale, formal process had never been attempted before the pilot.

As designed, the Observation-Coaching strand consists of three components: a preobservation conference, an observation, and then a postobservation conference. Specifically, the model asks that the mentor and novice teacher select an area of interest together, and then devise a method to collect data about the target area. Following the observation, the pair formulates a strategy to improve teaching, based on an analysis of the data. Although initiating this strand seemed ambitious, the challenge was to ensure face-to-face interactions between the teacher pairs.

Reflection Strand

It was critical to include a reflection strand, to promote the professional growth of the mentors. To do this, a graphic organizer, created by Germaine Taggart (1998) and based on Dewey's Theory of Reflection, was used to train mentors in systematic reflection. The basic components of this model include the following: (1) narrating the problem or episode in context; (2) framing and then reframing the problem; (3) forming a possible set of solutions or interventions; (4) experimenting with a selected solution; (5) evaluating; then (6) either accepting or rejecting the solution by virtue of the experimentation.

The Point of Convergence: Working with Andrew

The initial mentor-training session in August not only set the framework in place for the pilot program but also the basic expectations for the school year. As mentor coordinator, I had a firm handle on what to do. I suspected that the personal experience of working with a first-year English teacher would merge theory and practice. However, I had to be realistic. Were the expectations of the program practical, given the demands of our respective teaching schedules?

In August, Andrew and I began our mentoring relationship by working together for a full afternoon. We focused on organizing his curriculum units for the entire month of September, writing welcome letters to all of his sophomore and senior students, and finding manageable ways of controlling the "unwieldy," yet purposeful, journal assignments from students' summer reading. Although I suggested that he vary his method of assessing assignments, Andrew insisted upon giving points for all written classwork and all homework assignments, as well as all major essays. This meant reading every paper, every day. Soon, Andrew learned about the intense paperload of an English teacher, and it began to frustrate him.

From Andrew's perspective, there simply "weren't enough hours in the weekend" to get all of this paperwork done. I assured him that much of his first year would be spent "managing" paper and fulfilling daily requirements. There was no question that Andrew was in the "survival" stage. However, I encouraged him to use a Socratic Seminar rubric to grade class discussions. I also encouraged him to begin to count in-class assignments more easily with an index-card system. Over time, Andrew overcame the frustration of paperwork and felt more in control of his work.

We then chose to tackle other areas of concern through classroom observations. Andrew felt that perhaps he was standing next to particular groups in his classroom, while avoiding others. I designed a grid that duplicated the seating arrangement in his senior academic English class. For 20 minutes, I noted on the grid exactly where he stood. The data spoke volumes to Andrew. He was indeed favoring one particular group over the others.

In another lesson, I scripted all of Andrew's questions over a period of 20 minutes. This time, we discovered that most fell into the "What?" category. To work on higher-order thinking skills, I suggested that Andrew develop lists of

Essential Questions, based on the work by Grant Wiggins (2000). Clearly, Andrew was moving out of the "survival stage" and into the "teaching situation stage." Both of us began using Essential Questions on *The Great Gatsby* with our senior classes. By virtue of our conversation and reflection, I was beginning to see the dual benefits of mentoring. My lesson plans were improving as well.

From Pilot to Institutionalized Program: Standing the Test of Time

Explosive Growth

South Brunswick, located in central New Jersey, is one of the fastest-growing communities in the state. As a result, managing explosive growth while maintaining high-quality programs for our children remains our top priority. Since the pilot began in the summer of 2000, nearly 300 classroom teachers have been trained in South Brunswick's mentoring program to serve the burgeoning number of first-year teachers who are recruited to teach in our district. In the first year alone, over 115 experienced teachers served as mentors to our first- and second-year novice teachers in the program. Each year, our numbers grow, and, at this point, nearly 50% of our professional staff is nontenured. In essence, South Brunswick is a perfect place to look at mentoring, because it is an ongoing and critical support component of our recruitment and induction efforts across the district.

Our cadre of mentors has been called upon frequently to work with beginning teachers, and many of these experienced teachers have enjoyed this function as a part of their professional growth. Often, mentors report that this opportunity, especially the peer-coaching experience, has offered them a chance to articulate best practice in ways that they were not previously conscious about. As nurturing individuals, they look forward to sharing not only their lesson plans but also what they have learned over time. Others have stated that they are energized by the enthusiasm of their novice teachers and have learned about new strategies from these recent college graduates. In turn, these ideas have been explored in veterans' classrooms as well.

In our feedback sessions, mentors state that they spend most of their time working on plans together and discussing solutions to classroom management issues. Our more experienced mentors, however, have taken their work outside the ordinary. For example, some have planned joint professional days with their novice teachers. Mentors find that these opportunities to learn about, and experiment with, new ideas together are among the most valued experiences of their year.

I, too, remain steadfastly committed to mentoring newcomers to our profession and understand that our work as mentors directly affects the future of the teaching profession. As such, I continue to serve as the mentor coordinator for the district and, by virtue of this position, have witnessed the successes and failures of the program throughout its evolution.

Learning from Failures

One of the chief obstacles in overseeing this particular program is the fact that this is only one part of my district responsibilities; it is not my sole focus. An additional challenge is that we mentor teachers in 10 buildings over a 42-square-mile township. Over the course of the first year, we held regular feedback meetings with all of the teachers across the district to form recommendations for next year's program. Over the years, however, it has become increasingly difficult to maintain personal contact with the pairs, and I have relied on building principals to value the work to sustain the relationships. Relying on support at the building level, in some cases, has been most problematic for many reasons. First of all, the principals and supervisors are not entirely vested in a caring, confidential relationship between the mentor and novice. This should come as no surprise to experienced program directors, since none of the building administrators was included in the design and implementation of the program during the pilot phase. Therefore, administrators did not "buy in" as much as we would have liked. Proof of this rests in their reluctance to support the district's budget for a second year of mentoring when New Jersey reduced its funding.

Lack of administrative support was also evident in some areas at the building level. For instance, mentors often reported that they are unable to get release time from their administration to visit a novice teacher's classroom. This is a requirement of all mentors in the district. When asked, many principals stated that they felt as though the Board Office was handling "all of the mentoring."

Although I was initially discouraged by their less-than-enthusiastic response, I found that this obstacle provided a new opportunity to help the program become more meaningful to principals and supervisors. I decided to move our program from one that was basically a "broad brushstroke approach" for all to one that could be tailored by principals, based on their individual teacher's needs. I have since acknowledged this flaw with administrators, and I now continuously offer them my support for a tailored program. I have worked to include building principals in designing all future elements of the program. For example, two elementary schools are sending mentor-novice pairs to participate with Rider University in their new mentoring initiative called the "Virtual Learning Community" (VLC). Through a grant provided by the National Science Foundation, the science and education departments at Rider have forged a collaboration to support new, experienced teachers through Internet-based coaching. The fundamental idea of this project is for elementary science and math teachers to explore mentoring through the lens of inquiry. VLC involves university faculty, industry scientists, mentors, novice teachers, and others to learn about science and mathematics "without the constraints of time and space." All of us are excited about this opportunity and look forward to a second year of virtual mentoring.

Administrators do, nonetheless, understand the importance of mentoring support, but it is not necessarily a priority. And, since we are hiring up to the first day of school, some novice teachers do not receive a mentor assignment. It is critical that every novice teacher has the support of a mentor from the outset.

With increased involvement on the part of administration, the programs at each level are becoming more personalized and, therefore, more valued by administration. I am pleased to say that, despite this initial failure on my part, our partnership for mentoring continues to grow.

Not Getting Along

Unfortunately, failure of the mentoring process sometimes occurs at the personal level. Although principals match mentors and novice teachers with the very best of intentions, some pairs simply do not get along. To counteract this problem, we have created a "no fault dissolution" policy. This means that any mentor, or any novice teacher, may change the match if either one desires—no questions asked. A notion such as this has been one of the hardest ones for excellent classroom teachers to accept because of their drive to succeed, and for some administrators to accept without explanation. Nonetheless, if a mentor or novice teacher wants to change, we find another mentor. In one situation, a novice teacher's colleagues treated her unfairly in public. The mentor felt unable to defend her novice, and was unwilling to continue to support the new teacher because she was risking her acceptance within her department. I immediately recruited another mentor who willingly helped the novice through this difficult period. Although the novice teacher was not invited to return to teach in our district, the mentor supported her as she changed her career plans and found a new sense of self. I am convinced that this young individual and her mentor will be friends for life.

Learning from Success

Although there are some difficulties, in most cases, mentors and novice teachers report favorable views, with the novice teachers reporting that they were grateful that they could go to someone for help without feeling as though they were imposing on busy colleagues. More importantly, mentors and novices told us that there are four criteria to a successful mentoring relationship. These criteria are:

1. a willingness, on the part of the mentor and the novice, to embrace the benefits of the mentoring relationship;
2. proximity in the building to facilitate face-to-face interactions;
3. similarity of teaching assignments to facilitate collaboration of curriculum planning and sharing of ideas; and
4. time allotted from the administration to accomplish the objectives of the mentoring program.

None of this surprised me. The data the teachers reported reflected the sentiments that Andrew and I shared in our conversations. If the mentor and the novice teacher truly wish to participate in the relationship, most will overcome obstacles to realize the benefits of mentoring.

Summary and Conclusion

Several essential questions emerge from this work that continue to be our guide as the South Brunswick Schools' program changes and grows. These questions are:

1. What is the efficacy of the mentoring program in South Brunswick?
2. How does this process support and sustain the novice teacher?
3. Will novice teachers remain in this profession because of their mentoring experience?
4. How does this process energize the veteran teacher?

There is no question that South Brunswick was fortunate to have been selected as a pilot district. The state's initiative provided funding and an outstanding opportunity for us to intensify our mentoring efforts. We were also given an opportunity to develop quality professional development activities for a large segment of the professional staff. The program improved the mentor teachers' overall knowledge base about the skills needed to provide expert mentoring. We hope that our novice teachers' abilities will be enhanced, and they will remain teachers in our district.

And I have been fortunate, too—not simply because of my involvement in the program, but also because of my work with Andrew. Clearly, the convergence of these two perspectives provided a unique vantage point from which to view this process we call mentoring. It is important, because our mentors are becoming more skillful, nurturing, and reflective. Their efforts assisted our novice teachers' induction into a challenging and demanding profession. And, the fact that the results of this work will be shared with schools means that others will benefit well beyond the boundaries of South Brunswick.

The good news is that Andrew, like many of his colleagues, has become a tenured teacher in our district, and he will mentor a novice teacher this school next year. I am delighted to see this next generation of mentors offer "professional, confidential, and caring support" for an inexperienced teacher. Thus, the definition that we used for the pilot program continues to serve the district well. And, Andrew has made his transformation from "self as student" to "self as teacher" by way of entering The Student Concern or Mastery Stage. I have witnessed Andrew's process of moving through his stages of concern. Both Andrew and I value the benefits of our collaboration, and I am anxious to hear about his experiences. In many ways, Andrew's professional growth has enriched my professional life.

Last March, New Jersey's Commissioner of Education, William J. Librera gave a keynote address to over 100 attendees at our Mentor–Novice Teacher Reception. The purpose of the reception was to acknowledge the work of our mentors, and to share some of our mentoring experiences in different schools. Librera acknowledged the work we do in South Brunswick and stated that our commitment to mentoring does not occur in all school districts. He also stated that if teaching is to become a "true profession like law and medicine, then professional talk among teacher colleagues needs to become a formal part of the work day." We must do all that we can to challenge one another's thinking. Further, the commissioner is developing new plans to train teachers from preservice through accomplished teaching. Mentoring is one element that will be a part of the plan. In addition, the Department of Education, the New Jersey Education Association, and The New Jersey Principals and Supervisors Association are also collaborating to energize and sustain the work of mentors statewide. However, because of the budget crisis in New Jersey, funding for a formal mentoring program beyond the first year has been eliminated.

In spite of the persistent challenge posed by the national trend of teachers leaving the classroom, we are determined to attract, and keep, qualified novice teachers in the profession. However, we cannot provide mentoring in name only; all of us must do this work in earnest.

Acknowledgment

Sections of this chapter have been previously published in *The Virginia English Bulletin* (Volume 52, Number 1; Spring 2002).

References

Anderson, E. M., & Shannon, A. L. (1988). Toward a conceptualization of mentoring. *Journal of Teacher Education, 39*(1), 38–42.

DeBolt, G. P. (Ed). (1992). *Teacher induction and mentoring. School-based collaborative programs*. Albany, NY: State University of New York Press.

Taggart, G., & Wilson, A. P. (1988). *Promoting reflective thinking in teachers: Forty-four strategies*. Thousand Oaks, CA: Corwin Press.

Wiggins, G. (2000). *Understanding by design*. Pennington, NJ: Relearning by Design.

Wollmer, S. J. (2001). Turning back the turnover tide. *NJEA Review, 74*(9), 11–18.

For Consideration:

1. Do you think that the definition of mentoring for this district is adequate and helpful? Explain.
2. How can mentors and mentees use the coaching strand to improve classroom teaching?
3. Note one significant difference between the mentoring program described in chapter 2 and this mentoring model.
4. Name and explain one significant similarity between the mentoring program described in chapter 2 and this mentoring model.

Chapter 4

Teacher Initiation and Mentoring: Learning from Business Organizational Models

Alyce Hunter

The initiation of teachers into the culture of a school can be enhanced by learning from and using the theories, ideas, and models espoused by business organizations. Mentoring, learning from seasoned members of the organization, is one of the essential ways that newcomers, whether they are business employees or teachers, discover the culture they are about to enter. This organizational culture can be defined as

> the patterned ways of thinking, feeling, and reacting that exist in an organization (Tosi, Mero, & Rizzo, 1999, p. 353).

Furthermore, culture, whether it is that of a business or a school, can be identified by considering the basic values that it views, consciously and subconsciously, as important. These values are demonstrated in the actions and reactions of the organization as an entity, and of the powerful individuals, such as peer leaders, supervisors, principals, and administrators. Most importantly, for new teachers, these values are the basis for judgment, by peers and supervisors, of their actions and teaching performance. Tosi et al. (1999) identify six ideas, the response to which form the basic values of an organization. These are how the organization views and values: (1) innovation and risk-taking; (2) stability and security; (3) respect for people; (4) outcome orientation; (5) team orientation and collaboration; and (6) aggressiveness and competition. This list of six values can be used as conversation topics between individual mentors and their mentees. They can talk about what each of these concepts means in general, and specifically, in relation to their school. For example, a formal definition of the term can be followed by the mentee sharing what he or she thinks the concept might look like. The mentor can follow up with specific examples of the term demonstrated in their school. Then, both can discuss how the mentee can "fit" into, and work with, this cultural norm.

As the director of staff development, which includes a mentoring program, I begin to "enculturate" during new-teacher orientation (which mentors are invited to attend) by explaining how the school's mission statement was the result of a collaborative effort of community members, administrators, parents, teachers, and students. Next, I give everyone (mentor and mentee) a copy of the statement, and we read it chorally all together:

> The West Morris Regional High School community will provide students with an intellectually challenging experience that promotes a passion for learning, academic excellence, involved citizenship, and personal responsibility. This experience will foster the development of creative, confident, compassionate, and resilient individuals.

We talk about specific words, such as "passion," and what this means and says about us as a school. After the discussion, we read it again. This final choral reading can have the effect of establishing for the new teachers, and of reestablishing for the mentors, the organizational values implied and stated in the mission statement. This sharing of ideology moves toward creating a covenant—an agreement between all members of the school community. This sharing of ideals can help the new teachers understand, and fulfill, their obligations toward themselves and their new school.

Not only can the school's culture and values be clarified for new teachers through the use of ideas and models from the business world, but these ideas and models can also provide further insight into how a school culture is transmitted and maintained. Bowditch & Buono (2001) contend that, for an organization to be healthy, myths and heroes are essential. Myths are stories about the organization, including such tales of how it was founded or how it survived troubled times, that encompass the actions and reactions of "larger-than-life" heroes. Such myths and organizational heroes are manifestations and symbols that help transmit, and carry on, a culture. The sharing of myths and tales not only reinforces cultural values but also gives new teachers descriptions of how things are, could, or should be done. Identifying and celebrating organizational heroes helps new teachers not only understand and appreciate the school's past history but also set a standard for performance and motivation. Mentors can help in this cultural transmission by recounting stories of their own first days of teaching, including their foibles but emphasizing their successes. Mentors and mentees can then gather together to talk about what they learned about each other, and the school, through this storytelling. This storytelling expands from the mentor's obligation to include the organizational responsibility for the transmitting of values and norms. For example, during the first day of our initial mentoring, training includes a tour of the school building, with an emphasis on the plaques that have been placed in various classrooms to honor the teachers who have retired. Student tour guides regale the new teachers with tales of the history teacher who taught not only them but also their parents and grandparents! This telling of tales about successful teachers serve to set a standard for, and to provide motivation to, the fledgling teachers. Additionally during the new-teacher orientation days, various administrators and teachers will tell stories to the group about their own experiences during the "good (or not so good) old days." Laughter is mingled with respect as those new to the profession, or to the school, hear gray-haired peers tell about their exploits. Though our school has not done this as yet, the writing down or recording of these stories would certainly create a lasting memorial and history of the school and its culture. Additionally, some veteran teachers will share letters written to them by students and parents, and will proceed to tell about what happened to this writer. Such letters, and subsequent comments, not only continue the school's "story" but also personify the belief system of the reader and the school. To help mentees relate the concepts of myth, heroes, and history to themselves, they are asked to write (for their own eyes only) a description and explanation of what their legacy will be. How will students be different because they had Ms. or Mr.____? Will the school be different in 1, 5, 10, or 20 years because the mentee taught there? This sharing of myths, history, letters, and dreams helps new teachers to relate to the organization or school and to clarify for themselves their own goals, as well as the relationship between these goals and those of the school.

Furthermore, continuing to apply business organizational models to school organizations and communities, one needs to consider that

> the best way to ensure that cultural communications are credible and suc-
> cessful is to back them with consistent actions and behaviors that corre-
> spond to the espoused beliefs and values (Bowditch & Buono, 2001, p.
> 296).

In other words, how do schools and mentors not only communicate to mentees but also, more importantly, show them what is important and valued? With regard to new teachers, schools, as organizations, display their culture and communicate what is important and valued through the recruitment and selection process, the orientation procedures, and career development opportunities.

The recruitment of new teachers needs to aim to produce the selection of new employees who are predisposed to the school's beliefs, values, and culture. Specifically, candidates who are comfortable with, and will benefit from, a mentoring relationship with peers should be sought. To find such employees, Byars & Rue (2004) suggest that "job analyses, human resource planning, and recruitment are necessary prerequisites" (p. 135). The objective is to find, from a pool of applicants, the teacher who can teach most successfully and can fit into, yet help, the existing school culture. Schools, like businesses, need to use multifaceted criteria to narrow the pool of prospective teachers. Teacher application forms that reflect the school's goals and objectives are essential. For example, if a school professes to value communication—specifically writing—then a writing sample should be required on the application. Moreover, the writing assignment can be tailored to reflect the school's essential values. For example, the basic question, "What is your philosophy of education?", can be modified in a school where mentoring is vital, to ask, "What is your philosophy of education? Be sure to include not only how you feel about students and subject matter but also how you feel about collaboration and cooperation among teaching peers." These application forms can then be screened for those who work well with others and are willing to listen to, and learn from, mentors who are not in supervisory or evaluative roles. Preliminary and secondary face-to-face interviews should continue to ask questions, to probe for how the prospect will work with peers. Prospective mentors, particularly those with prior mentoring experience, can be involved in these interviews. Additionally, just as business organizations do, schools can present realistic job previews (RJPs) to prospective teachers. RJPs can include written documents (school report cards, newsletters, etc.), visitations to classrooms, conversations (not interviews by) current staff, and introductions and interactions with prospective mentors. Furthermore, RJPs, by providing realistic communication about teaching and school expectations, can be an important part of initiating and socializing prospective teachers. New teachers need to know what will be expected of them, so that they can make an accurate appraisal of how they would "fit."

In addition to learning from business organizations about the recruitment and selection of new employees, schools can look to these organizations for ideas about effective orientation, the formal and informal introduction of new employees to their organization, and their job. Byars & Rue (2004) maintain that it should be a shared responsibility, within an organization, to introduce new workers to both the general aspects of the organization and the demands of the specific job. Mentors, as guides and veterans, can—and should be—involved in both aspects of orientation. For example, in my school, our formal orientation day for new teachers involves both mentors and mentees. This joint day is considered essential, so that mentors will literally hear the same thing as new teachers do about the school and performance expectations. The mentors themselves have been through a training experience prior to this. Their training experience is conducted by mentoring coordinators, who themselves have been, or are, mentors and are teachers in the school. These coordinators design the mentor day to include such topics as defining mentoring, identifying the skills, qualities, and abilities of mentors, understanding new-teacher needs, talking about ways to develop effective relationships and to establish trust, and so forth. Mentoring is presented as a positive way to impact the school culture and community. However, difficult issues, such as when and how to intervene if the mentor feels the mentee is not performing successfully, are also discussed. Finally, mentors are encouraged to contact their mentees, through e-mail, phone calls, or face-to-face meetings, prior to the formal orientation day. Therefore, mentors are prepared to be vital contributors during this first formal training day.

In our school, this training day has taken a variety of forms and formats, as it continues to be reflected upon and refined from year to year. Such reflection and refinement are the results of the feedback we get from new teachers at the end of the day, and at the end of their first year of teaching. Additionally, the written reflections on the day, and on their overall experience, provided by the mentors enlighten plans for the next training day. Finally, a mentoring committee, composed of the mentoring coordinators and administrators, meets to look at the feedback and reflections, and to modify segments of the day. Our training day began as a series of lectures, punctuated with films and group discussions about what constitutes good teaching. The afternoon was devoted to mentor and mentee meeting together privately to work on lesson plans and subject-area expectations. While acknowledging that the lecture method does promote clear and consistent understanding among new teachers and mentors, that the discussion method validates the voices of both the experienced and the inexperienced, and that using films effectively reinforces the good teaching practices expected of new teachers, the mentoring committee, this past year, concluded that our orientation day did not really reflect our culture. We wanted new teachers to have an experience, and to learn about our school, through our beliefs and values. Consequently, administrators, teachers, and students planned a day to challenge the new teachers to go beyond—to establish high expectations for themselves and their students. Student leaders led the new teachers and mentors through a variety of Project Adventure–type activities. Trust falls and blind walks began the day, as new and seasoned educators put their trust in students to lead. Other activities included a tour of the building led by students. During this tour, mentors and mentees were reminded of the history of the school as they stopped by various classrooms and were told about the "legends" who had once taught there. Administrators shared stories about their own first teaching days. Teachers and administrators read letters from students who expounded on their high school experiences and, particularly, their teachers who had helped them to succeed. Other physical challenges, such as scaling the wall that required teamwork, ended the day. Our unconventional training day was validated when I overheard an experienced teacher who was to teach at our school for the first time remark, "Can we do this again? I learned so much about what your school really is, who I really can be, and the importance of working together."

However, as Byars & Rue (2004) assert

> It is virtually impossible for a new employee to absorb in one long session
> all of the information in the company orientation program (p. 189).

In our school, mentors collaborated with the mentor coordinators to develop a list of topics for further discussion and presentations. Formal presentations on peer-observation expectations and strategies were asked for, and attended by, both mentors and mentees. Second-year teachers were asked to, and did dramatic vignettes on, discipline issues frequently encountered by first-year teachers. The second-year teachers followed up each vignette with a discussion about the best way to address the issue. The vignettes ranged from the comical—how do you deal with a student who answers his cell phone while you are being observed by your supervisor?—to the serious—how do you deal with a student who confesses to you that he or she is using drugs? Coming together for an evening of popcorn and soda to view the movie, *Mr. Holland's Opus,* created a bonding between mentors, mentees, and administrators as they used the movie as a reference to discuss what constitutes good teaching and the process of becoming a teacher. Lunch meetings were held with the group of mentors and mentees to gauge group progress. Conferences were held with mentoring pairs to gauge their personal progress and relationship. First-year teachers themselves are provided in-service time to meet with each other and talk about the mentoring process and share mutual concerns and successes.

Moreover, mentors are not just involved in orientation activities. They are also an integral part of the career development of the mentee. For example, both parties collaborate on the planning binder that the school requires from each new teacher. This binder is more than a lesson-plan book. It contains such items as curriculum topics and timelines, unit and daily plans, handouts, activities, assignments, classroom rules and procedures, grading systems and rubrics, and communications between parents, administrators, and the new teacher. The mentor and mentee collaborate to collect these artifacts. Also, they reflect on the success or failure of the practices and actions these artifacts represent. This planning binder is a dynamic record of a teacher's first year. It is used as the basis for their second year of teaching and also as a start for their teacher portfolio. This portfolio requires them, as second-year teachers, to select from this collection, the artifacts that they feel represent them best as a teacher. These artifacts are formally presented to administrators as an added dimension to the evaluation process.

Applying concepts and ideas learned from business organizational models can help schools refine their current practices, with regard to recruitment, orientation, and career planning for new teachers. Schools can look to these models as they work to institute practices that celebrate their own unique culture.

References

Bowditch, J. I., & Buono, A. F. (2001). *A primer on organizational behavior*. New York: John Wiley & Sons.

Byars, L. L., & Rue, L. W. (2004). *Human resource management*. Boston: McGraw-Hill.

Tosi, H. L., Mero, N. P., & Rizzo, J. R. (1999). *Managing organizational behavior*. Malden, MA: Blackwell.

For Consideration:

1. Explain how mentors can be involved in recruitment, orientation, and career development for mentees.

2. Identify and explain one concept or idea that schools can learn from business organizations.

3. Consider the mentoring programs described in this chapter and in chapters 2 and 3. Comment upon how mentoring is a way to create a teaching and learning community.

Section III

Mentoring as a Way to
Transform Teaching and Learning

Chapter 5

It Started with A Phone Call: The Process of Mentoring

Todd Toriello

"A thousand roads diverged in a yellow wood and I, I took the one modeled by my mentor, and that has made all the difference."

—Robert Frost

What It Means, How It Works, Why It Serves

The phone rang one August morning as I contemplated my entrance into the world of high school teaching. The voice on the other end was a friendly one, almost childlike, in fact, a voice that would soon become my guiding force in a sea of uncertainty, trepidation, and high tides. It was a voice that was highly invitational, incredibly upbeat, and undeniably sincere. It was a voice that promised support, presence, and guidance. It delivered in ways that far transcend the parameters of healthy collegiality. It was the voice of a mentor, my mentor, one who grew to become one of my most treasured teachers, most trusted peers and, perhaps the richest dividend of all, most respected friends. Thank you, West Morris Central High School, for my mentor. They do not come any better.

I begin with my mentor because she represents the catalyst into a larger system of mentoring that literally wraps its arms around novice teachers and provides them with the fuel to grow, to risk, to reflect, sometimes to fail, and always to stand up and try again; a system with continuity and ongoing assistance; a system grounded in research; a system that creates a culture for professional development; a system anchored by sound, responsible, professional supervision; a system focused on the fundamental competencies of effective teaching; and finally, a system predicated on a set of goals that clearly challenges the novice teacher, professionally and personally, to develop within a context of maximum support. So, to those who ask, "What is mentoring?", the answer, to me, is *a process that guides and supports the novice teacher in a systematic, specific, collegial partnership necessary to acquire and maintain professional excellence.* The operative word is process. It is *not* a person, a place, or a thing. Rather, it is an ongoing journey of support. With the right kind of response to that support, a response grounded in seriousness of purpose, the novice teacher is invited to experience a privileged opportunity—becoming part of an initiative that breeds exemplary teaching and exemplary teachers. Students deserve nothing less. What does this process look like, and how does it work?

When I reflectively examine the mentoring process at West Morris Central, what I see is an exemplary lesson plan delivered by exemplary teachers who understand, right down to the belly button, what exemplary instruction is all about. That is the way I perceive the process—as a superb lesson. Allow me to explain why. Suppose, for a moment, that someone from a foreign land arrived on our soil with no knowledge of our system of education. Suppose that person posed these questions: How would I know good teaching when I see it? How would I identify a good teacher and good instruction? Those of us with proper training would answer those questions with a rather common voice. Our words may be different, but core values would undoubtedly surface. We would say to our foreign visitor things that sound something like this:

- You would see highly invitational people inviting everyone in every class to learn.
- You would see people who know that their work is continuous, never finished.
- You would see common foundations across all disciplines—people who plan and who prepare, people who care about "the environment" of their classroom, people who differentiate instruction and engage students in the "construction" of their own learning, people who modify and accommodate to serve the needs of all, people who frame lessons around multiple intelligences, people who engage students in such a way that they (students) become the worker, the doer, people who avail themselves of professionally expanding opportunities as the natural order of things.
- You would see multiple opportunities at every turn—at the assessment level, at the planning level, and at the instructional level.
- You would see positive encouragement and ongoing support.
- You would see people going the extra mile to serve.

These are the types of responses our foreign visitor would hear.

In a very real sense, the West Morris mentoring process replicates the above description. The process is highly invitational and draws every new teacher close into the circle. The process is ongoing. The process is meticulously planned, and the architects responsible for it are thoroughly prepared for its delivery. The environment for delivery is well constructed, engendering an atmosphere of trust, risk-taking, mutual exchange, and ongoing collaboration. There is ample opportunity to expand, and participate in, professional development activities. Positive encouragement is the only kind in town here. Finally, service from supporting colleagues by going the extra mile is a certainty. In short, the process looks very much like a splendid lesson, with a splendid teacher at the helm. It works because of its solid plan, its clear blueprint, and is both well conceived and systematically implemented. The blueprint, in all of its component parts, is well delineated, and each component compliments the others. There is a genuine choreography at work. Permit me to define the dance.

In the interest of specificity and organization, I shall reference the following five dimensions: (1) the actual orientation program; (2) the professional support by way of colleagues; (3) the professional development opportunities; (4) the professional evaluative framework; and (5) the individual focus area of the novice teacher.

Firstly, the actual orientation program for novice teachers in West Morris immediately sets the stage for the kind of professional tenor and landscape new teachers can expect. Unlike many school districts that offer a one-day orientation for new teachers, literally burying them in a sea of paper and procedure, West Morris offers a program over multiple days. As a result, novice teachers are active participants in hands-on activities, discussion groups, collaborative sharing, and focus sessions. Additionally, strong engagement of the participants is modeled each day. This multiple-day approach affords opportunity for teachers to digest the material presented, to meet many district leaders, to get to know each other, the facility, and the myriad of details necessary for new teachers to master. By the end of the multiple-day sessions, some significant bonds have formed that a one-day orientation would not permit.

Among the most powerful forces at the orientation program, in my judgment, is the "type" of material forming the backbone of the orientation. By type, I mean the *substance* of the material itself. Never once do the presenters merely fill the room with rules and procedures we could otherwise have read on our own. Instead, the substance of our future professional life is the focus. We hear of the district's broad-based mission, we learn of the belief system that anchors our learning community, we are presented with descriptors of effective teaching, with fundamental competencies that West Morris expects of its teachers, with plans on how to manage a classroom, especially on the first day of school, with discipline guidelines, and with the overarching goals that give structure to mentoring. These are the types of things under scrutiny. Through these discussions, we, as new teachers, come to realize early on what West Morris values in teachers and in teaching. An entire sensibility is thus established during the orientation. The days themselves are held together with a very clear and present attitude—that we are here to bring something extraordinary to students. The encouragement to do so is palpable.

Additionally, for novice teachers at West Morris, the strength of the orientation sessions is matched by the strength of professional collegiality rendered by those around us. I call it a gift. I briefly referenced my mentor earlier in this chapter. From the moment she contacted me in August to introduce herself as my assigned mentor, her support never ceased. Not only did she meet with me during the late summer to chat and to offer some preliminary advice, but she also remained my support system on a daily basis. Specifically, Michele assisted me with lesson planning, lesson pacing, assessment techniques, material selection, exam development, core standards, and grading. She modeled lessons for me and offered to observe my lessons, in an effort to give me feedback. In watching her, I was able to identify the kind of teaching skills I wanted to emulate. She willingly shared materials, assessments, and approaches that worked. Her orientation was forever positive and her professionalism unyielding. On a personal level, she helped to integrate me into the Department of English, always applauding my efforts and always believing in me. In the process, I became a believer in me as well. She truly served as a role model, whose availability and accessibility were one and the same.

In addition to a formal mentor, West Morris provides the novice teacher with much ancillary support as part of its overall mentoring program. During year 1, my lead teacher served as a trusted companion, assisting me at all levels. No question was ever too small or too large for Ralph. He responded to my expressed needs with grace, often with wit, and always with encouragement and confidence. His constant help gave me an opportunity to understand the culture of the English department in particular, and of the broader school community in general. Regardless of the area, be it materials, curriculum focus, assessment, or instructional strategy, he was there as both advisor and confidant. He, thus, became a paragon for me. Today, he remains so; and I am the richer because of my association with him.

Moreover, a team of professional evaluators serves as another dimension of collegial support. This team, consisting of the director of professional development, the director of curriculum, and the principal, formed a trinity of professional assessment in my behalf. With their help in preconferencing, classroom observation, and postconferencing, I was able to critically assess myself as a teacher. Their feedback was invaluable. Add to them an administrative team and a faculty that respects new teachers and willingly responds to their needs, and the novice teacher is left with one word to describe the collegial relationship—supportive. Thus, the mentoring is both formal (through the mentor-mentee relationship and the evaluation team) and informal (through the willingness of others to respond).

Also central to my novice experience at West Morris is the extensive array of professional development experiences to fuel my needs as a teacher. I vividly recall the director of staff development reviewing the smorgasbord of opportunity available to me—from conferences, institutes, study groups, online workshops, courses, and curriculum activities, based on standards, technology training, and problem-based learning. The opportunities seemed endless; and I quickly learned that my "master teachers," if you will, were ready to provide me with ongoing options for growth and development. I felt both grateful and charged to participate.

The professional evaluation framework is yet another dimension within the overall mentoring program, one that aims at creating excellence in teaching and learning. As a novice teacher, I learned that professional evaluation in West Morris provides a system of professional assessment that demands rigorous teaching standards and offers differentiated professional growth options. The fear factor, the one-size-fits-all model, the nonspecific checklist—none of these have become part of the West Morris protocols for professional evaluation. Instead, based on the descriptors of effective teaching as presented to us during orientation, the teacher experiences levels of development and pathways to growth. Again, growth is continuous and dynamic; and teachers are invited to experiment and grow within the pathways to excellence. Reflective practice guides the process. The entire framework provides additional guidance and support to new teachers. Today, three years after my beginning, now the director of professional development encourages these same values with new teachers, guiding them with both care and grace.

The final dimension to be referenced here is what West Morris calls the "individual focus area" for professional growth. For the novice teacher, the development of a Professional Portfolio or Planning Binder is the requirement. For the first two years of teaching, a Planning Binder, reflective of all lesson plans, handouts, assessments, related research, unit strategies, and teaching materials, is a mandate. Through the compiling of this planning binder, I was able to better understand all of the descriptors of effective teaching as presented. The binder became my own resource not only for teaching and organizing, but for reflecting on my own practices as a new teacher. This binder thus became my professional growth plan as a beginning teacher, setting the stage for me to consider future plans in my later years of experience.

To review, the mentoring process at West Morris is broad-brushed in its scope, multidimensional in its opportunities, and authentic in its spirit. How it serves the novice teacher is directly connected to its essential mission—to support in such a way that new teacher success is the outcome. Through the mentoring process, the novice teacher knows from day 1 that an entire system of support is scaffolding his or her efforts. That system is machinelike in that all the gears work in tandem to move the newcomer along a continuum of growth—the orientation process, the collegial relationships—such as the mentor-mentee marriage—the professional development opportunities, the evaluative framework, and the professional learning focus. The whole then becomes a direct reflection not merely of the *sum* of its parts but rather of the *integration* of its parts. It garners its strength of service to new teachers because the machine presents in working order, functions in working order, and sustains itself in working order. The process thus becomes a great deal more than a mentor meeting with a mentee. What it becomes is a full-scale new teacher-induction program that clearly engages new teachers in a dynamic, ongoing process. It, therefore, models the very principles that give it life—truly a constructivist system. Additionally, the new teacher is surrounded by professionals who not only value and encourage new teacher contribution but also invest an inordinate amount of time and energy to both create and deliver a training ground anchored in a sense of excellence, professionalism, and shared responsibility. Thus, the vision and the promise of the superintendent, shared at the time of hire, is redefined. It's quite a blessing.

The real magic, however, is simply stated. The process serves because it is real. This is *not* a process that merely fills the documentation mandates for public education. Instead, it opens itself to those wonderful forces of professional partnership, letting new teachers know that their jobs are awesome, their responsibilities far-reaching, and their possibilities endless. At the same time, it lets new teachers in on a great secret—that there are *no* secrets to success in our profession, but rather skills, competencies, values, and boundaries, all springing from the expectation of incredibly hard work and ongoing professional commitment. It serves because the process "walks the walk." As one who, not long ago, received the invitation to enter the West Morris arena and begin the journey, the walk, still going on for me on a daily basis, represents one of those privileged opportunities of my life; and yes, it started with a phone call.

It seems appropriate to conclude this discussion on mentoring by focusing on its outcomes—the real substance of why we do what we do. When I consider why mentoring serves, I am, of course, drawn to a host of obvious reasons that lend credibility to the process. I, and probably many relatively new teachers, having recently navigated the waters of mentoring, could generate a list that might reflect many commonalities that serve young educators: (1) identifying skills and practices that breed excellence; (2) developing professional knowledge and attitudes relative to core content standards, classroom management, parental interplay, instructional strategies; (3) understanding special-education issues; (4) integrating new technologies; (5) understanding interdisciplinary stands; (6) encouraging collegiality, risk-taking, and professional reflection; (7) enhancing collegial relationships through peer-to-peer support; and (8) growing through sound, responsible evaluation frameworks. The list could go on and on, in direct proportion to the breadth and depth of the mentoring program itself.

For me, however, the mentoring process at West Morris Central, in addition to the obvious, as referenced here, has provided some far richer rewards. If Shakespeare was right when he suggested, ". . . ambition should be made of sterner stuff . . . ", the administration in my district took him to heart when crafting its mentoring program. The architects of my program and the incredible people delivering it—my mentor, my lead teacher, my administrators, my evaluators, my staff developers—all came from a deeper place than the obvious. Yes, they provided a framework to walk me through those early, confusing, overwhelming days; and grateful I am for those supports. But, in doing so, they presented me with the power of their own example. That is the key answer of why the process served me so well. By watching them as they revealed themselves—as teachers, as colleagues, as professional partners, as human beings—I was able to live a vision I only thought I understood. I quickly learned that I understood only the surface of things. It was when they freely opened their classroom doors, their briefcases, their filing cabinets, their bags of tricks, their honest, open wells of experience and knowledge, and their hearts and souls, that I began to truly understand what this wild and wonderful career of teaching was all about. As a novice teacher in a mentoring program, I was part of a process whose organizational principles were anchored in demanding the best of its people. Anything less was unacceptable. Through mentoring, West Morris modeled that standard in a clear, pervasive voice—through orientation, through daily contact with my mentor, through unbelievable help from my lead teacher, through sound evaluation, and through ongoing staff development opportunities. What I gained were all of the "building blocks" of teacher survival. But what I lived were those deeper, richer acknowledgements that help us, as young teachers, to create our own visions and our own philosophies of teaching—the kind that make us who and what we are. I shall be forever grateful for those building blocks; but I shall feel forever blessed for the philosophy I presently embrace, one that I trust will mature and deepen through the years as I reflect on my beginnings. It is with extreme gratitude and profound respect for all that West Morris afforded me through its mentoring program that I formulate and share a philosophy of teaching that speaks to the program's lessons, its standards, its people, and its spirit.

I have always believed that any philosophy of teaching in particular must be an outgrowth of a philosophy of education in general. Having said that, I turn to one of my literary heroes, the French essayist, Montaigne, who says it best in his essay, "Of the Education of Children."

> . . . for it seems to me that the first lessons in which we should soak his
> mind must be those that regulate his behavior and his common sense, that
> will teach him to know himself and to live well and die well.

Inherent in that bit of philosophy is the challenge that education presents to me as a teacher: to expose children to alternatives for living healthy and productive lives. Whether it be through the classroom situation, the field-trip experience, the extracurricular activity, the community resource contact, or otherwise, education, in my judgment, is an ongoing process that must provide a variety of broad-brushed experiences to better help children know themselves within such contexts as their strengths, their weaknesses, their fears, their uncertainties, their individual expectations, and, most of all, their individual feelings. I have come to understand that exemplary teaching must sensitize children to themselves and to the world around them. If the broad, long-range goals of education are ever to be realized, if the rather esoteric statements of educational philosophy are ever to be seen as practical and reasonable (i.e., the dignity of the individual, the perpetuation of a democratic society), then teaching, in my mind, must concentrate its efforts on providing society with good, solid human beings—human beings who, through each new experience, each success, each failure, are developing a positive self-concept; human beings with a desire and an ability to contribute; human beings who are willing to accept civic responsibility; human beings who are sensitive to themselves and to others; human beings with a thirst to find new answers; human beings who accept and know how to provide criticism as well as praise; human beings who can recognize the need for improvement and act; human beings who can recognize or accept another's recognition of their own weaknesses and their own strengths; human beings who have the courage to say, "This is the way I believe"; human beings who recognize the need for and the power of literacy as a vital social tool; human beings with a respect for the world of which they are a part and an ambition to make it even more respectable; human beings with convictions, ideals, and purposes; human beings who will allow themselves to "get involved"; finally, human beings who, in response to Montaigne's first lesson, will "know themselves and live well and die well."

In order to truly live the philosophy as defined here, a classroom needs to become a learning laboratory, and the teacher needs to work to develop a culture and a climate in which to articulate standards—standards of conduct, standards of academic achievement, and standards of attitude. In connecting to all three, I develop, for myself, a stronger philosophy of teaching.

Regarding standards of conduct in a classroom, the concept of mutual respect anchors my philosophy. As a teacher, I believe the presence of respect fuels the classroom positively, while its absence serves as a major impediment. For me, respect is the crucial force behind trust and human interplay. A teacher who demonstrates, and actively acts on, respect for students will usually find that respect returned in the classroom. Through active listening (listening as often as we speak), through going beyond the surface of students' lives and attempting to know them outside of the classroom walls, through empowering student initiative and supporting decision making, through establishing reasonable boundaries—student to teacher, teacher to student, student to student, through honoring diverse ideas and alternative approaches, through allowing mistakes and utilizing them to learn rather than to punish—all of these practices engender respect and create a climate in which respect becomes the required expectation in the classroom.

Standards of academic achievement, for a teacher, are imperative for classroom definition. Philosophically, I believe it is important to articulate these standards in a variety of ways, such as in both writing and presentation to students and in a follow-up to parents, so that home and school communication is clear. Standards, in my judgment, should link to the specific achievement mandates, as defined by state and local testing, and should also provide for differentiation of instruction in order to meet the diversity of abilities and special needs, some of which may be deeply personal. At the same time, I, as a teacher, need to set diverse standards and define them with clarity to my students. To design a "one-size-fits-all" set of standards is to negate a host of individual differences within a classroom. Therefore, as a teacher, I subscribe to the required benchmarks for a grade level, but to a diversity of approach and a range of accommodations and modifications to meet the complexity of needs within a classroom.

Finally, standards of attitude are central to my philosophy of teaching. It has been said that "people seldom improve when they have no other example but themselves to copy after." The implications of that concept form the basis of my philosophy of teaching with respect to standards of attitude. In specific terms, I see teachers as leaders who set the example, who exemplify the example, and who teach by the example. In doing so, a value system is brought to the classroom and becomes the classroom culture. The culture carries with it specific voices that anchor my philosophy of teaching. The voices are distinctive: School climate, primarily influenced by teachers, is a number-one priority in the overall spectrum of school life, achieved, for the most part, through mutually honest and authentic interactions; professional growth is enhanced through an open, honest support system that reaches in and reaches out; schoolwide visibility is an absolute teacher imperative; a humanistic approach to problem solving lends itself to increased productivity in a classroom; giving credit where credit is due enhances growth through a sense of shared success; the classroom is a "team," where every member counts and where every member needs to feel significant; a meaningful alliance with parents is a teacher's lifeline; a systematic approach to problem solving is a teacher's must in a classroom.

As a relatively new teacher, if I find the wisdom to live this philosophy as I create my future classrooms, then I may one day have the privilege of affirming the words of Montaigne. I see that challenge as both a mission and a mandate; and the mentoring process at West Morris Central frames and fuels my pursuit.

For Consideration:

1. Explain how a mentoring program can be "broad-brushed in its scope, multidimensional in its opportunities, and authentic in its spirit."

2. Explain why it is important for a mentoring program to be "broad-brushed in its scope, multidimensional in its opportunities, and authentic in its spirit."

3. How has being mentored transformed this author's perception of teaching, in general, and of his own teaching, in particular?

Chapter 6

Mentoring North Carolina Novice Teachers Training Program: Lessons We Have Learned

Ted S. Henson

North Carolina's Excellent Schools Act, landmark legislation passed in 1997 to improve student achievement, called for revising the state's 12-year-old Mentor–Support Team Training Program. The following year, a new program with a new name, Mentoring North Carolina Novice Teachers (MNCNT), was introduced in the schools.

The design and content for the Mentoring North Carolina Novice Teachers training program was generated through the collaborative efforts of a statewide committee that included representatives of local education agencies, institutions of higher learning, the North Carolina Center for the Advancement of Teaching (NCCAT), retired educators, national induction consultants, and the Department of Public Instruction, with geographic representation from throughout the state. MNCNT contained six modules, totaling 24 hours of instruction, to prepare teachers to serve as mentors.

The first module, *Induction*, provides an overview of the state's mentoring program and considers the needs and roles of novice teachers and mentors. The second module, *Concerns of Novice Teachers*, generates a list of concerns facing the novice teacher and provides activities and discussion items that ask the mentor to reminisce about their own first year, and to create a profile of a successful novice teacher. Module 3, *The Role of the Mentor*, draws examples of mentors from children's literature, identifying the qualities of an effective mentor, and considering ways to apply these qualities to support new teachers. The fourth module, *Communication*, concentrates on the skills of good verbal and nonverbal communication. Module 5, *The Reflection Cycle*, demonstrates an effective model for reflecting on current classroom practices and designs a plan for growth based on that reflection. Finally, module 6, *The Coaching Cycle*, details effective coaching strategies for the mentors.

Worthen & Sanders (1987) stated that one serious defect in most new educational programs was the lack of evaluation. They pointed out that program evaluations hold one of the greatest promises for reform in education. Evaluations provide the information needed to make changes in the education system. Without serious evaluations of a program's effectiveness, educators simply follow the path of randomly adopting the current educational trends.

With this in mind, NCCAT, a partner in producing the training module, conducted an evaluation of MNCNT in 2000. Participants in the original field tests of MNCNT, who were now training teachers with the instrument, were asked to complete a survey rating the effectiveness of the training, and to make suggestions for future improvement. The information gathered provided valuable information toward putting together programs for beginning teachers and mentors at NCCAT.

The comprehensive evaluations of MNCNT showed that the teaching strategies and activities were its major strengths. These activities generated group discussions, which ranked as the second-strongest component of the training. During the discussions, participants were able to draw from their own experiences, and to apply new information learned from others.

The Coaching Cycle, based on a model of continuous improvement, was the highest-rated module. In *The Coaching Cycle*, mentor teacher and novice teacher thoroughly discuss the beginning teacher's teaching process. The mentor observes and documents the process, and together they reflect on the process. Decisions can then be made that strengthen the novice teacher's professional development. Research has shown that, as a result of this observation, documentation, and reflective process, the mentor teacher also grows professionally (Huling-Austin, 1990; Garmston, Linder, & Whitaker, 1993; Lee & Barnett, 1994).

Survey respondents also rated *The Reflection Cycle*, *Concerns of the Novice Teacher*, and *Role of the Mentor* as strong elements of the program. *The Reflection Cycle* module was closely tied to the Performance-Based Licensure Program (PBL). At that time, all initially licensed education personnel (ILP) were required to successfully complete the PBL to obtain a continuing license to teach in North Carolina. The respondents stated that, if mentors are to effectively help their novice teachers achieve continuing licensure, they must first understand the PBL program and its requirements.

The basic insights into the purpose and nature of mentoring, included in *Concerns of the Novice Teacher* and *Role of the Mentor*, were other program strengths. Mentors receive training in mentoring techniques they can use in various situations that may arise while working with a novice. These modules provide information to strengthen the effectiveness of the mentor in responding to the needs of the novice.

Module 1, *Induction in North Carolina*, was noted for including the Interstate New Teacher Assessment and Support Consortium (INTASC) standards.

The INTASC standards provide a framework for mentors to use in evaluating and assisting ILPs in North Carolina.

At the time MNCNT was written, the final guidelines for Performance-Based Licensure (PBL) had not been developed. This limited the amount of information that could be included in the training program. Since a major role of the mentor in North Carolina is to guide the novice through the licensure process, the basic guidelines should be included into the mentor's training. Respondents gave three suggestions for accomplishing this:

1. Novice teachers are currently required to write reflections on instructional practice, needs of a unique learner, and the classroom climate. Specific training in writing such reflections, using the questions from the PBL Handbook, would better prepare mentors in assisting novice teachers.

2. Mentors need comprehensive training in the process of Performance-Based Licensure. The three components of the revised PBL should be explained in detail during mentor training, rather than waiting for the mentors and novice to learn about them at the same time. This would give the mentor an edge in preparing the novice for the process of obtaining a continuing license.

3. The program would benefit from the use of videos demonstrating teaching practices by novice teachers. The videos would provide opportunities for observations and reflections based on actual classroom situations. Adding videos to the training program would address another limitation pointed out by two respondents, who asked for more real-life examples of the needs of novice teachers.

The survey respondents also noted that a successful mentoring program requires administrative support and recommended that local administrators complete the training along with mentor teachers. Other respondents' suggestions were for specific grade level and for information on the research-based classroom. While both of these suggestions have value, they would be difficult to incorporate into a statewide program. Since MNCNT is designed to meet the needs of mentors at every grade level and in every local education agency (LEA), suggestions for specific grade levels or programs should be considered at the local level.

Recommendations

The extent of this program evaluation is limited by the newness of the program. At the time the surveys were administered, the program had only been in use for one year. This study can report only on the short-term outcomes, as reported by the survey respondents. Additional evaluations should be conducted to determine the mid- and long-term outcomes of MNCNT.

Since the length of the initial licensure period in North Carolina is three years, it would be appropriate to conduct another program evaluation at that time. The novice teachers who were assisted by mentors trained in MNCNT could be asked to rate the effectiveness of their mentors. However, the researcher must keep in mind that, the further a survey is done from the initial mentor training, the more likely other factors will influence the outcome.

To maintain the timeliness of MNCNT, the program should be updated when related programs are revised at the Department of Public Instruction. For example, in 2002, the North Carolina legislature suspended Performance-Based Licensure while conducting a study to determine the feasibility of continuing the program. If major changes are made in the licensure process, MNCNT must be revised to remain relevant to mentor needs. Without revision, the effectiveness of MNCNT would be greatly diminished.

Mentor training programs are works-in-progress. They must be continually updated to meet the ever-changing challenges facing beginning teachers. Frequent program evaluations and revisions will help assure effective training. It is helpful for groups involved in the revision of statewide programs to become involved in joint collaboration to discuss common issues. Such beneficial sharing of information provides a seamless continuum of information for the training programs being developed.

References

Garmston, R., Linder, C., & Whitaker, J. (1993). Reflections on cognitive coaching. *Educational Leadership, 51*(2), 57–61.

Huling-Austin, L. (1990). Teacher induction programs and internships. In W. R. Houston (Ed.), *Handbook of research in teacher education* (pp. 535–548). New York: Macmillan.

Lee, G., & Barnett, B. G. (1994). Using reflective questioning to promote collaborative dialogue. *Journal of Staff Development, 15*(1), 16–21.

Worthen, B. R., & Sanders J. R. (1987). *Educational evaluation: Alternative approaches and practical guidelines*. New York: Longman.

For Consideration:

1. Rank order the six mentoring modules, according to how useful you believe each would be to a new mentor.

2. Why is evaluation of the entire mentoring program essential?

3. What aspects of the North Carolina mentoring model do you believe have the most power to transform teachers and teaching? Explain.

Chapter 7

Mentoring Teachers: Five Stories

John R. Maitino

At 11:30 a.m., four weeks after the quarter had begun, and 60 minutes before she was to teach her eigth grade English as a Second Language (ESL) class, Sylvia is told by her cooperating teacher and the school principal that there are problems with her work at the school. She is not showing much initiative, her dress and personal hygiene are unsatisfactory, and her teaching is "over the heads of your ESL students." It is a difficult, at times, excruciatingly painful meeting, one that I attend as her university supervisor.

What quickly emerges is a complicated situation in which perceptions differ sharply, only five weeks remain in the quarter, the cooperating teacher is clearly overextended in her responsibilities, and Sylvia is emotionally unprepared for such harsh criticism.

The resolution of Sylvia's problem came slowly, somewhat agonizingly, over the next eight weeks, and got me thinking about the business of mentoring student teachers. Tidy resolutions don't always emerge from complicated human problems. And supervision models applauded in respected journals sometimes collide with the hard realities of classroom teaching, offering little guidance. What I want to do below is to sketch brief portraits of five student teachers and reflect on the ways in which their personal qualities helped to shape each of those mentoring relationships.

The moment of decision about what I will do most often comes when I plan the observation or meeting with a student teacher. I ask myself questions about her or him to determine appropriate strategies and relating behaviors. Is she motivated to deal with the situation? Does she have confidence to change or adjust her teaching? Does she understand her strengths and weaknesses? Does she learn from her own experience? Sylvia's problems, described above, offer an example.

Directive Mentoring: Fixing Problems

(Glickman, Gordon, & Ross-Gordon, 1995, p. 9)

When we met directly after the 11:30 a.m. meeting to discuss the situation, I said we had two options—find another school or continue at the same school, with the obvious advantages and disadvantages. Sylvia wished to stay, and I suggested we find a second cooperating teacher. We did, one who provided a more accommodating environment and accepting attitude. But the more important issue, the criticisms, needed airing.

Some context on Sylvia is required. I had known her for two years through classes and advising. She had worked hard, earning a bachelor's degree in English in a rigorous program, all the while supporting herself and her daughter. She was determined to meet her goals, including a teaching credential and job, and the financial independence that would follow. At the same time, however, she appeared, on occasion, embattled in personal relationships that she did not always understand, and was given to doubt and depression.

When we discussed the criticisms, Sylvia could find no basis for any of the comments in either her teaching or her personal behavior. I suspected interpersonal conflict in the relationship with the cooperating teacher, and believed Sylvia was emotionally ill-equipped to understand, or resolve, the problem. Consequently, I suggested we write up a plan to address each criticism and talk weekly after the observations about progress in those areas. The plan involved three elements: (1) share with the first cooperating teacher specific, agreed-upon goals as a guide for daily teaching (my suggestion); (2) emulate the dress and appearance of teachers at the school (Sylvia's idea); and (3) simplify English as a Second Language (ESL) lessons with a breakdown of tasks and strategies (cooperating teacher's suggestions).

As it turned out, Sylvia did the best she could. She taught scripted, if uninspired, ESL lessons; she dressed with a more colorful and professional appearance, which seemed to give her a certain pride; and she made measurable, though modest, progress in her teaching under the guidance of the second cooperating teacher. Eventually, she found full-time employment in teaching.

What Sylvia did not, and probably could not, do, given her limitations, was utilize problem-solving strategies to discover and develop a full range of teaching skills. In his very helpful book, *Mentoring New Teachers*, Hal Portner (1998) suggests that supervisors and mentors must, with unmotivated or unwilling teachers, focus on behaviors which "fix" specific problems (p. 60). I very consciously chose to use a highly "directive" approach in my relationship with Sylvia, sensing in her limited self-awareness and interpersonal skills, an inability (or unwillingness) to evaluate her teaching or even use constructive suggestions. I could only hope that Sylvia would begin to discover in this very prescriptive process a method for developing viable teaching strategies.

Collaborative Mentoring: Solving Problems in Tandem

Andrea walks briskly back and forth in the front of the classroom, firing questions at random students, following up when an answer demands clarification, her eyes everywhere at once. The questions, and especially the follow-up questions, reveal her command of the subject—Act I of Shakespeare's *MacBeth*—and a sense of the interpersonal dynamics of this classroom.

Andrea's voice is sharp, sometimes insistent, always driven by conviction, enthusiasm, and a sense of purpose. As the lesson unfolds, with students alternately reading aloud from Act I and responding to questions on meaning and tone, I have a strong impression of a motivated teacher with a dramatic presence and a sense of timing, who knows where she is going.

In contrast to my discussions with Sylvia, my post-lesson conferences (and e-mail chats) with Andrea quickly evolved into collaborative conversations about the lesson. For example, with both student teachers I used an observation technique called the "anecdotal record" (see the Appendix of Observational Strategies for extended definitions of this, and other, strategies), in which you write down, in short sentences, a description of a particular student. Each sentence becomes a kind of discrete observation, which allows one to get a sense of what particular students are doing, and of the temporal flow of the classroom (Acheson & Gall, 1980, p. 120).

While Sylvia would rarely interpret the meaning of the anecdotal record, Andrea offered quick takes on any number of these short observations. For example, I wrote, "Jesse (a female student) turns her eyes back to the instructional handout when you say, 'You in or out, Jesse?'", and Andrea said, in response to my anecdotal record, "I have to keep reminding Jesse and her little coterie of associates to stay on-task." When we reviewed a series of such anecdotal observations, recorded over several lessons, I would ask if there were one or two patterns that might help us focus on "important moments" in her teaching, moments which, if we thought about them long enough, might lead to the most significant positive changes in instructional practice. Andrea identified class management and putting more responsibility for learning on the shoulders of the students.

We developed a succession of strategies for each area, which Andrea used in class over the coming weeks, and what emerged was a continuing discussion of the relative merit of these approaches. For example, Andrea began to set clear behavioral limits, apply them in class, and note improved time on-task among students. I asked, in one observation, when a student mimicked her disciplinary approach, what she thought her "sharp voice" and "abrupt manner" telegraphed to students. "Does it serve as a cautionary warning, a highlighting of the moment, or what? What will be its effect on behavior when it is done over several weeks?" She was not sure, but did not see in the next three weeks a letting up of mimicry or other occasional manifestations of disrespect.

We finally developed a very concrete plan for evaluating student behavior and appropriate responses to it. I suggested that Andrea do the following for a specific class: (1) Visualize all the acceptable behaviors you want, and write them down; (2) Observe and record unacceptable behaviors; (3) Develop and apply specific strategies to eliminate unacceptable behaviors; and (4) Reevaluate each strategy after one week, and revise or adopt a new strategy. Over 13 weeks, Andrea used a series of strategies, including behavioral and instructional approaches (from adopting a reserved demeanor to overplanning lessons), which slowly improved classroom behavior, but did not eliminate all, or most, unacceptable conduct.

In the end, Andrea's capacity for self-critique, and her willingness to experiment, allowed for collaborative mentoring, where we identified problems and developed a variety of strategies to solve those problems. Andrea's own evaluation of this collaborative relationship came in an e-mail composed a year after her student teaching ended, when she had been teaching full-time for about seven months. In part, she wrote:

> I think I benefited most by you staying after the observation to discuss my strong/weak points. Keeping track of the time on your observation allowed me to see how well paced the lessons were. As for our weekly journal entry, it was nice to rant and rave as well as take pride in the successes.

My own notes identify "marker periods of discovery and growth in (Andrea's) teaching," both through our collaborative work (the four-step visualization strategy discussed above) and through my more traditional evaluation of her teaching ("set specific limits and enforce them . . ."). Arthur Blumberg & Edmund Amidon (1964) offer possible reasons for such growth in a review of teacher perceptions of supervision. "The researchers made an interesting discovery: Teachers felt they learned most about themselves, as teachers and as individuals, from conferences high in indirect and direct supervision" (p. 1–8). It may be that the collaboration (indirect supervision), which teaches problem solving, helps teachers to evaluate their instructional practices in a more objective light and use critical evaluation (direct supervision) to their advantage. In any case, Andrea benefited from a mentoring style that included collaborative as well as directive elements.

Nondirect Mentoring: Facilitating Self-Reliance

> The first classroom observation ends, Patti announces we cannot conference now, so I ask her to e-mail me a response to my written notes, and I will call her the next day. Her e-mail says, among other things, that she will devise a way of calling on more students, because she noticed, from my observation, that she called on a small number of students, some of them repeatedly. When I call on the phone, she is not available.

> Seven days later, the second observation takes place, and I write two comments in my notes. "One: You called on 32 students in the first 35 minutes,

and actually called on each one at least once, it seemed. Impressive. Two: What did you like the best that happened during the class period, and what would you change (and how)?"

Though I had assigned another supervisor to observe Patti during the semester, I visited her twice because she was a member of the seminar on student teaching I directed. She was clearly eager for my visits, and every bit of "criticism," as she called it, that I might offer. She was an emergency credential teacher, which meant she was teaching a full load with no training, extra observation, or advising from the school site where she worked.

During the first visit, I used a "verbal flow" observational strategy, which records who is talking and to whom, categories of verbal interaction (i.e., teacher question, student answer, teacher praise, student question, etc.). This technique gives an objective record of the verbal nature of the lesson in many of its particularities (Acheson & Gall, 1980, p. 105). Patti noticed, without my prompting, since we could not meet after the lesson, that she only called on eight students, some of them repeatedly. Before my next visit, she had experimented with two ways of increasing the number of students who answer, settling on a technique of using individualized name cards to guarantee that she called on most, if not all, of her students. During the first half of the second visit, the discussion unfolded as a fast-paced exploration of a short story, its plot, and significant themes. The use of the cards greatly increased the number of participants, and enhanced the attention of almost all class members.

In the second observation, I recorded "directions and structuring statements" as close to verbatim as possible, the time given, and the context in which they were delivered, so that their relation to the class lesson would be evident (Acheson & Gall, p. 93). Typical of Patti's structuring statements was the following, given directly after a minilesson, in which effective dialogue and correct use of quotations was taught: "Now we will do a practice exercise, with you revising paragraphs and adding quotation marks." (She asks several questions of Ginny, Tom, and Jose, checking for understanding before she moves on.) She then continues, "You take words in the paragraph, and you make dialogue. Remember, you copy and revise it, adding the quotes where they are needed." Students then worked individually, with Patti checking their progress, and concluding the lesson with student examples on the overhead.

When we met after the lesson, I asked Patti how she felt about student learning during the lesson. She said, "I felt they had a grasp of how quotation marks show who is speaking, but I wondered whether I should have intermittently put individual student examples on the overhead throughout the lesson, and discussed them one at a time, instead of doing a whole group all at once. What did you think?" I said that she should assess their work the next day to verify what they actually learned, but also thought the idea of "intermittent" examples with discussion could only help to reinforce learning.

Patti was clearly the best equipped (of the three student teachers discussed so far) to use my observations as a springboard for analyzing her lessons and teaching strategies. She used my first observation (without a postlesson conference) to adopt a question-asking strategy, which immediately improved engagement and on-task behavior among students. And, after the second observation, she was able to engage in a kind of reflective questioning, in which she stood outside of herself to critique the lesson and offer alternative approaches of high quality (Lee & Barnett, 1994, pp. 16–21).

Nondirect Mentoring: Growing but Risk-Taking

A plank rests on the floor in the center of the classroom, a scarf neatly folded on one end. Students step over, or around, it as they walk to their seats, at the same time avoiding Dan, the student teacher, who stands just to one side of it. I am filling in student names for the "At-Task Seating Chart," an observational strategy, which charts whether and when students are on-task.

The bell rings. Dan abruptly and loudly snaps his fingers, saying, "I need three lightweight girls for an experiment. Four guys." The girls volunteer, are sent out of the room, and Dan explains that each girl will be blindfolded, lifted on the plank 6 or 8 in, then lifted a few more inches, each time believing she is being lifted 1½ ft.

I put aside my observational strategy a few minutes into the experiment, sensing it was irrelevant to the drama unfolding before us. Dan guided each of the three girls through the experiment and later two boys, talking to each, peppering them with questions about their reactions. Students watched and listened. He turned to the audience, asking (as one blindfolded boy stood inches above the floor, but seemed to believe he was much higher), "Why am I doing this?" Then, without warning, he stopped the experiment, and asked all students to describe in writing what had taken place: blindfolded students narrating in first person their individual experience, and audience members capturing events as they witnessed them.

The lesson, it turned out, was a prelude to a class discussion of a scene in a short story, in which a character finds himself on a narrow ledge in danger of falling to his death. Personal observation and (blindfolded) participation naturally enhanced student attention to the story's language, narration, and irony, inviting rich comparisons between student writing, on the one hand, and the short story writer's well-crafted narration, on the other hand.

When we met after the class, I shared my reactions as follows: (1) lesson creates high level of interest via observation, personal participation; (2) interactions are fast-paced, student-centered, with strong interest in what students think, see, do, and write; (3) scaffolding of plank activity with student writing and analysis of story scene guaranteed intense interest in writing and reading; and (4) when you say, "I need more focus over here," or "Stop packing up," you are wisely demanding their full attention, a reminder of how important each moment is.

Dan had a remarkable gift for engaging his students in sustained critical reading and writing, coupled with an intense desire to grow as much as he could as a teacher. His focus on inquiry, problems which students find powerfully interesting, the careful scaffolding of those problems for deep and sustained critical thinking and writing, and the movement from more to less teacher control—all of these carefully conceived strategies led to an intensity of student engagement in learning I have rarely witnessed in my career as a teacher and supervisor of student teachers. Larry Johannessen (2001), in a recent *English Journal* article, argues that such instructional practices help students "learn the kind of strategies that will enable them to be productive citizens now and well into this century" (p. 45).

While I occasionally offered Dan suggestions, such as put the burden on students to ask questions you are asking or make them identify the specific writing or grammar problem, I always felt I was just dropping small pebbles in a large pond with little substantive effect.

When he completed his credential, I found ways to involve Dan in teacher training, and saw more exemplary lessons and units, but also hints of risk-taking, which caught my attention. One involved an "into" activity for teaching Golding's *Lord of the Flies*. He brought his own students to a summer institute for teachers, and had the students engage in an adaptation of the Milgram experiment. A female student was instructed as part of an "experiment" to deliver small electrical shocks to another student, and to increase the voltage when Dan instructed her to do so. She complied with little hesitation, despite growing expressions of concern and heightened physical reactions on the part of the student receiving the shocks. (In reality, no shocks were administered, the experiment being an attempt to measure whether and how far a person will go in following the instructions of an authority figure.)

While the activity provided a very engaging introduction to *Lord of the Flies*, a small number of teachers that day raised questions about the ethics of involving an unsuspecting student in a test of her willingness to engage in "questionable" behavior. Those concerns got me thinking about Dan's risk-taking, the student's rights, and the value of using unconventional strategies in a time when students seem less willing to engage in genuine reading, writing, and thinking.

I also asked Dan to perform the plank lesson in a student seminar, and inquired, in the course of recreating the lesson, what precautions he took to assure that students were not hurt. Dan said that a student had once hit his head on a desk, but new procedures now kept desks away from the student, and more students surrounded the plank.

On two occasions after the Milgram and plank lessons, I told Dan that he might be putting himself into jeopardy because of the risks which come with some of his lessons, and that he should give consideration to ways of modifying, or eliminating, such lessons from his curriculum. He was a credentialed, tenured teacher, but I knew he would listen attentively to my suggestions, because he always took our conversations seriously. Nevertheless, I found it very difficult to question a mature adult (38 years old), a professional of considerable accomplishment, whose classroom I had not observed for several years. I am not sure now whether changes were made, but feel strongly that Dan deserved my honest and best judgment.

Mentoring: Failure and Some Redemption

A gifted writer and articulate and sensitive reader of literary texts, Mark finds himself unable to earn his secondary credential in English. During his first student-teaching assignment, one of his two master teachers removes him from one class because of serious class-management problems. In his second student-teaching assignment, the middle school principal removes him from all student-teaching duties after Mark pushed one student and dropped another's books on the ground in front of him.

As the credential coordinator and Mark's supervisor, I recommend to the Teacher Education Department that he be terminated from the program, due to temperament problems and a continuing inability to establish effective classroom management procedures in his teaching assignments. A committee overrules my recommendation, and asks me to establish a remediation program, including another opportunity to student teach.

While I felt strongly that Mark was unsuited for secondary school teaching, both for reasons of temperament and weak social skills, I asked him to undertake the following steps: (1) remove himself from any secondary school experience for three months; (2) observe and work with (and be mentored by) an effective English teacher for a period of two months, while substitute teaching; and (3) successfully complete a quarter of student teaching under two cooperating teachers. I reasoned that the time away from school would provide perspective on past problems, while mentoring and observation might strengthen confidence and provide a foundation for building teaching and management skills.

When Mark began student teaching again, I was acutely aware of the problematic relationship we shared. Supervision, as Cogan says, "is psychologically . . . almost inevitably viewed as an active threat to the teacher, possibly endangering his professional standing and undermining his confidence" (Acheson & Gall, 1980, p. 6). As his supervisor, I set clear boundaries, specific and reasonable expectations, and sought to mentor him through relating, assessing, coaching, and guiding (Portner, 1998, pp. 6–8).

In the end, however, Mark lost the confidence of his cooperating teachers, and was unable to effectively manage, or teach, his four classes. When I met with him during his final week of teaching to let him know he would not earn the credential, I knew it would be a terribly difficult encounter. I was determined to state the facts as I saw them and help Mark understand that this disappointment could, in time, assist him in setting a new course in his life.

As we sat in his classroom, I quietly told Mark that his evaluations identified "serious" problems in management and teaching, which had persisted during each block of student teaching. I said that he would not receive the credential because he had not been able to manage or teach his students independent of his cooperating teachers. He began to argue, blaming the two current cooperating teachers and me, and refusing to allow me to continue. I insisted that he let me finish, and told him something I truly believed. "You have one of the most analytical minds I have seen in my 24 years as a teacher, and a way with words that is remarkable. If I saw you walk out of one of the towers downtown (Los Angeles), wearing an expensive suit, and you told me you were a lawyer with one of the big firms, I wouldn't be surprised." When my eyes reddened, he stopped me, saying, "My mother wants me to get the credential. I don't. I'm not good at teaching."

It was a telling moment because, when he saw that someone understood his situation, he seemed to be released from the failure he had experienced. We talked about what he would do next, what he had learned from the experience, and what strengths might help him in the future. It was a redemption of sorts, the best that could be taken from a bad situation.

Conclusions

In a curious way, the new or student teacher governs the mentoring relationship much as an individual's personality shapes the development of personal relationships. While the mentor can be a teacher, a sponsor, or a guide, he or she must also understand the student teacher's capacities, and take them into account in developing the relationship. I have found that when a student teacher's motivation and ability to address problems is limited, as in Sylvia's case, I need to spend more time nurturing trust and offering (and reinforcing) prescriptive strategies for fixing problems. On the other hand, motivated and skilled student teachers can assume greater responsibility for their own growth and development, allowing me to guide that growth through collaborative problem solving and reflective questioning. Such was the case, to greater and lesser degrees, with Patti and Andrea.

At the same time, Dan and Mark suggest, in different ways, the limitations of the approaches to mentoring relationships I have discussed here. In Dan's case, risk-taking was both a source of his greatness in teaching and a cause for concern. While I was able to confirm and reinforce his innovative approaches to instruction, I was never sure, in either direct or indirect approaches to mentoring, that Dan understood my concerns about his risk-taking as a potential source for future problems. It may be that the risk-taking is so much a part of his personality that he cannot conceive of undertaking effective instruction without it. So many of his lessons stripped away the vestiges of the traditional classroom—from blindfolded experiments to students as guinea pigs—that to "retreat" to the safer, if less psychologically and emotionally interesting, instructional model might threaten the genuine intensity and engagement his students experienced on many days.

In Mark's case, he was never to be a secondary teacher, but the more important question became his understanding of his failure to complete the program and earn the credential. When his frustration and anger erupted during the final meeting, I did not let any defensiveness on my part show itself, but did allow Mark to see that I felt badly and understood he possessed distinguishing intelligence and knowledge. I did not want to leave that room until he understood that much.

Appendix of Observational Strategies* ˙

Selective Verbatim (pp. 81–83): Make a written record of exactly what is said (verbatim transcript). Supervising teacher must agree on what to look for in lesson (keys are emphasis on verbal process in teaching, selectivity of focus, objectivity of the created record).

Asking Questions (pp. 83–88): This may be the single best technique, but its effectiveness depends on examining the teacher's intent for the lesson in which observation occurs.

Student Teacher's Directions and Structuring Statements (pp. 93–96): Record as close to verbatim as possible all relevant statements, time given, context in which they were delivered so their relation to class lesson, etc., is evident. Research shows that manner of directions, and whether they are given at all, has an effect on student achievement.

At-Task Technique (pp. 98–105): Using an at-task seating chart, in which you keep an ongoing record of student behaviors at selected times during the lesson. Though the correlation between at-task behavior and learning is not perfect, since a student may be on-task but confused and unable to master the lesson content, a focus on at-task behaviors gives the teacher and supervisor objective data, which may help to explain the quality and quantity of learning.

Video and Audio Recording for Microteaching (pp. 123–126): Video and/or audio recording is done of a microlesson, which may be defined as the student teacher practicing a few specific teaching skills in a scaled-down teaching situation of 10–15 minutes, with anywhere from 5 to the normal number of students participating. Data is objective (since it is visual and/or auditory and specific skills are the focus for a limited time period), giving the student teacher an opportunity to self-evaluate, identify strengths and weaknesses, and revise teaching approaches.

Observational Record (no source): Supervisor uses an observational record to record a lesson in its entirety through observation of as many relevant areas as possible. Objectivity is limited, though nonjudgmental language and focus on performance behaviors reduces subjectivity.

<u>Verbal Flow (pp. 105–110)</u>: Record who is talking and to whom; record of categories of verbal interaction (i.e., teacher question, student answer, teacher praise, student question, etc.). This technique gives an objective record of the verbal nature of the lesson in many of its particularities.

<u>Anecdotal Record (pp. 119–126)</u>: Records with short, descriptive sentences, each one summarizing a discrete observation. This technique is useful when student teacher cannot think of specific behaviors for observation, especially at the beginning of student teaching. The recorder should strive to be objective (for example, do not write, "you did a good job of . . ." but, instead, write, "teacher gives directions, asks for someone to put the directions in her own words, June does so."). The more objective the record, the more easily will the student teacher be able to form judgments on the effectiveness of the lesson and guiding of the student teacher.

* Page numbers indicate source in *Summary of Techniques in the Clinical Supervision of Teachers*.

References

Acheson, K. A., & Gall, M. D. (1980). *Summary of techniques in the clinical supervision of teachers: Preservice and in-service applications* (2nd ed.). New York: Longman.
　The authors summarize a host of valuable observation strategies, approaches to postlesson conferencing, among other ideas.

Blumberg, A., & Amidon, E. (1964). Teacher perceptions of supervisor-teacher interaction. *Administrator's Notebook, 14*, 1–8.

Glickman, C. Gordon, S., & Ross-Gordon, J. (1995). *Supervision of instruction: A developmental approach* (3rd ed.). Needham Heights, MA: Allyn & Bacon. I have adopted their styles of supervision, including Direct, Collaborative, and Nondirect.

Johannessen, L. R. (2001). Teaching thinking and writing for a new century. *English Journal, 90*(6), 38–45.

Lee, G. V., & Barnett, B. G. (1994). Using reflective questioning to promote collaborative dialogue. *Journal of Staff Development, 15*(1), 16–21.

Portner, H. (1998). *Mentoring new teachers*. Thousand Oaks, CA: Corwin Press. This short book is most helpful, providing a range of insights on relating behaviors, pre- and postconference communication, developing trust, and effective feedback strategies. I cannot recommend it too highly.

For Consideration

1. In the ideal world of the mentor-mentee relationship, mentors would be involved in observing their mentees actually teaching. Why are such observations important?

2. The author uses an observational strategy called "verbal flow." Define this strategy and explain how it might be used in a mentor-mentee relationship.

3. Explain how the "at-task technique" could provide feedback and discussion for the mentoring relationship.

4. How, in your opinion, does the relationship building, stressed in this chapter, transform teachers and teaching?

Section IV

Mentoring as a Way to Create
Partnerships in Learning

Chapter 8

The Superintendent Is a Vanishing Breed

Judith Ferguson

The superintendency is a high-stakes job with a great deal of risk. Fewer and fewer people are choosing this career that was once considered as a highly paid and respected profession. The crisis is exacerbated by the baby boomer syndrome. Nationally, it is predicted that 50% of those who now fill leadership positions are expected to retire within 10 years.

However, the baby boomer syndrome does not fully explain the shortage of qualified candidates for the superintendent position. As with any complex problem, there are many contributing causes to this crisis.

Women and minorities continue to be underrepresented, influenced, in part, by a lessening but still existing bias. While 60% of the people in the superintendent pipeline are women, only 13% are employed in a school-leader position. Minorities in this pipeline have increased slightly from 3.9%–5.1% over the last decade.

Search consultants report that premier districts that attracted over 100 applicants for superintendent positions in the past now feel fortunate to receive 30 qualified applicants, and many need to reopen the search in order to find an acceptable school leader.

Today's leaders face growing expectations for performance, often accompanied by declining human and financial resources to do the job. State standards and high-stakes testing have made school leaders accountable for results, yet boards of education frequently refuse to grant them the autonomy they need to do their jobs effectively.

The workweek for many school leaders is easily 50 hours, and some claim to work as many as 80 hours per week. The job is overwhelming, and the rewards are few. School officials are subject to public criticism that often borders on abuse. For this, they get paid only slightly more than the highest-paid teacher in the district.

The average tenure of a superintendent is less than three years. Many new school leaders minimize their exposure to risk by entering the superintendency later and leaving it earlier than did superintendents of the past. Another emerging face is the young and less-experienced candidate, who is now being selected by boards as first-time superintendents.

Board-superintendent relationships are, perhaps, the greatest impediment to attracting and retaining school leaders. Role confusion leads to micromanaging, and special interests often take precedence over best interests.

The issues that school leaders face today are increasingly complex and require solutions typically outside the expertise of a trained school administrator. Columbine is just one case in point. September 11th is another. One does not know, from day-to-day, what crisis may arise that requires immediate, and continuing, system intervention.

Why Mentoring Programs are Needed

Mentoring programs are an essential support system for new superintendents. If the profession is to attract and retain talented administrators as school leaders, it must support them through their initial years in order to make them successful.

Preservice and in-service programs are inadequate to meet the needs of new superintendents. Today's leaders must be able to grapple with issues that have no right or wrong answers. They regularly deal with paradoxes, dilemmas, and disputes. Yet, most graduate programs do not prepare them to be reflective practitioners who can handle these challenges. In-service programs, such as those available through state and national associations, are typically "shotgun" approaches that, research has shown, have limited value.

The superintendent is often referred to as the *Lone Ranger*. As author John Daresh (2001) notes in his book *Leaders Helping Leaders*, others view the superintendent in this way: "You're the boss. Fix your own problems, and don't ask for help from anyone. If you can't do the job on your own, you're a failure" (p. 2). Daresh proposes an alternative to the "sink-or-swim" concept, one that assumes that asking for help is an example of strength, not weakness. Mentoring is a key element of the professional development that one needs, and deserves, as a new superintendent.

Anyone who has been a superintendent knows that there is, literally, no one to talk to when one fills the top position. If the novice superintendent seeks help from a subordinate, he or she risks losing credibility as a leader. If he or she asks a board member for help, this may encourage micromanagement, and the superintendent's skills may be questioned. Although a network of superintendents is available through state and national organizations, this network has been historically viewed as favoring those who have been "in the system" the longest and have contributed to the organization through various leadership activities. Male superintendents continue to dominate state and national organizations. Although some state organizations have recently introduced programs for new superintendents, state associations, in general, are not viewed as "welcoming" by first-time superintendents.

The Practicum for New Superintendents— A Model that Works

In order to meet the unique learning needs of first-time superintendents and to increase their "staying power," in 2001, Citizens for Better Schools (CBS), a nonprofit New Jersey organization, launched a new program called Practicum for New Superintendents. As senior fellow for CBS, I became responsible for establishing and supporting this fledgling program that grew from two groups with seven new superintendents in its first year to 36 new superintendents in six groups by its third year! When CBS phased out of business in 2003, its leadership programs had become so well recognized in the state that leading organizations competed for them. The Practicum, along with a companion program for aspiring superintendents, has recently transitioned to *The Institute for Education Leadership, Research, and Renewal* (IELRR) at Seton Hall University.

The program design of the Practicum is both simple and powerful. Under the leadership of a highly experienced and competent superintendent, the new superintendent participates in monthly meetings of two to three hours, with a cohort of between five and eight peers. The leader conducts an initial intake session with each cohort member to establish a comfortable and meaningful relationship. At the monthly meetings, participants share experiences and find solutions to the challenges they face as new superintendents. Between meetings, help is available from the group leader through telephone and e-mail conversations.

Practicum leaders have found that topics of most interest and concern to new superintendents are:

- Dealing with difficult employees
- Handling of complaints
- Board-superintendent relations
- Managing the time demands of the job
- Dealing with the press
- Managing crisis
- Interpreting law and code
- Delegating effectively
- Acquiring and managing financial resources
- Leading change

In addition to the coaching, guidance, and support first-time superintendents receive from the experienced Practicum Leader, the program is designed to give them an immediate network of peers and a place where they can float "trial balloons" in a safe environment. The results are improved performance and increased job satisfaction, both of which lead to greater "staying power."

Between meetings, Practicum Leaders consult with group members as needed. Many report late-night phone conversations, often following a difficult board meeting. Some have made emergency visits to the district to help the new super-intendent with a particularly difficult problem. "Just listening" is perhaps the greatest contribution a Practicum Leader makes. Having someone available and interested is a real asset to a frustrated novice superintendent. Providing direct advice and sharing of resources are other ways that Leaders assist their group members during the year.

Leaders are encouraged to use a consultation model for group discussions. Each person shares a *real* problem, one of immediate concern or one recently experienced on the job. The novice superintendent takes about five minutes to explain the background, the players and the politics of the problem. He or she then discusses the options considered and, if relevant, the course of action se-lected. Next, members of the group ask questions for clarification and give feed-back. Feedback includes other alternatives to consider or examples of ways others have handled the situation. In no case is feedback judgmental!

In addition to learning more and improved strategies for problem solving, a direct benefit from group discussions is the "catharsis" that each member expe-riences by simply airing troubling issues within a safe and supportive environ-ment. It quickly becomes apparent that no problem is unique, that many new superintendents share similar concerns and challenges, and that there is no right or wrong way to tackle complex issues. What works in one setting may or may not work in another. What works for one leader may or not work for another leader. This realization is also comforting, because most new superintendents labor under the misconception that their problems are unique and that they must find the "right" solution or they will have failed. Learning to live with ambiguity is probably the most critical skill a new superintendent will acquire!

The Practicum further provides new superintendents with resources. As is-sues surface, group members begin to share resource information. A sample bud-get, a press release, policies, contacts, consultants, and so forth, are e-mailed, faxed, and Fed-Exed among the group members.

The value to the consultation model is that the fledgling superintendent ex-pands his or her repertoire of problem-solving methods and also learns to look objectively, rather than personally, at issues and problems. Some refer to this ability to step outside the problem as "helicoptering."

A surprise outcome of the program was the effect it had on the Practicum Leader. Those leaders who also teach at the university love the connection this program gives them to the real world of the school administrator. All consis-tently express the feelings of self-worth that come from helping others grow in the profession. As retirees, these former superintendents miss the positive feed-back they received from others, and now, as mentors and coaches, they feel needed and appreciated. The Practicum also keeps the Leaders abreast of issues and trends in education. They read more, and they think more than they might other-wise. NM says, "The Practicum keeps me at the cutting edge of the profession."

Another Leader with 53 years in education says, "It is nice to be useful at my age!"

In its fledgling year, the Practicum for New Superintendents served two groups, with a total of nine new superintendents. By the third year, the organization was running six groups in four different regions of the state, with a total membership of 34 new superintendents. At the close of the 2002 academic year, approximately one half of all new superintendents in the state had been enrolled in the Practicum.

New Jersey is a diverse state with over 600 school districts, including urban, rural, and suburban, ranging in student population from under 200 to over 30,000. The Practicum has attracted new superintendents from all types except the large, urban districts, which are few in number and, with few exceptions, are generally served by experienced superintendents. The AXA Foundation provides scholarship funds to support participation by superintendents who serve districts with limited financial resources. Many grants have been made to superintendents from small, rural southern New Jersey communities that struggle to fund their schools.

Recruiting Efforts

Finding new superintendents and marketing the Practicum to them has been accomplished in the following way. At the inception of the program, I, as senior fellow in charge of the program, delivered an information session for the 14 field representatives of the New Jersey School Boards Association (NJSBA), who conduct approximately two thirds of the superintendent searches in the state. Brochures were given to these field representatives who endorsed the program and recommended it to boards of education in their regions.

Annually, I secure a list of first-time, new superintendents from the New Jersey Association of School Administrators (NJASA). This list is provided to the four Practicum Leaders who contact potential candidates by telephone and/ or letter. The parent organization (now the IELRR) provides a printed brochure and an informative Web site for use by the Practicum Leaders in their marketing efforts.

Early on, however, participating superintendents voluntarily assumed a role in recruiting newcomers to the program. As first-time superintendents were hired in any one of the 21 counties, a program participant would tell them about the program and invite them to join. The combination of recruiting efforts works quite well.

Observing the Practicum in Action

Practicum Leader CH is a retired, highly successful superintendent with over 30 years in education. She started her career as a teacher and quickly moved up the ranks to superintendent. Serving as superintendent in a wealthy, suburban community for 10 years, CH faced many challenges, including overcrowded schools and a three-times failed building referendum.

CH's most recent group was comprised of six new superintendents from diverse backgrounds. Three served in K–8 districts with fewer than 1,000 students, two led K–12 districts in the medium-sized range, and another administered a countywide school district for special-needs students.

While this group of superintendents administered districts of varying sizes, shapes, and personalities, each shared the common ingredient of being new to the job. They also quickly learned that, despite the differences among their districts, the problems of first-year superintendents are strangely alike!

CH's group decided to meet at one member's district office each month. Her agenda typically combined a combination of individual problem analysis, with topics of interest such as budgeting, dealing with problem employees, and improving public relations. A few times during the year, CH invited a guest to share ideas and information. Guests were also experienced and successful superintendents with special areas of expertise.

Early in the year, one group member talked about her sudden and dramatic realization that the "buck stops here." As with every superintendent on September 11, 2001, this new superintendent dealt with the fears of students, parents, and faculty that resulted from the terrorist attacks on the World Trade Center and the Pentagon. Serving a district located in close proximity to New York City, the potential loss of loved ones was real, and the danger was immediate. No emergency plan, however current or complete, could anticipate an emergency such as this one.

In the same day that she was called to address the myriad of school issues related to the terrorist attack on the World Trade Center, this superintendent also received a bomb scare and had a fire in her building. "Everyone looked to me to take care of them," she said. "All of the service providers were gone. Police, fire, and rescue workers had flocked to New York City, and I was alone to deal with distraught parents, teachers, and students." One can be sure that emergency response was the hot topic when this group gathered for its next monthly meeting. Not only did the novice superintendents share their angst, they also shared their ideas and their crisis plans that followed.

Hearing her tell her story, I was reminded of my first year as a superintendent. Sitting in a session for new superintendents conducted by the Department of Education staff in Trenton, New Jersey, a two-hour drive from my school district, I received a call from my board president telling me that a student had committed suicide in a music practice room during class at the high school. I still remember the dread and fear I felt and the lack of confidence about what to do. During the drive back, I got my bearings back and, with the help of an experienced high school principal and a sensible board president, we put together an emergency plan to deal with press, parents, faculty, and students. I wish that I had had, at that time, an experienced superintendent to turn to for advice and council and a peer group to share my feelings with as well!

Despite the crises she has faced and the heavy load that she carries, this new superintendent still enjoys a honeymoon with her board and, as a former secondary person, she relishes the opportunity to work with elementary children and teachers. She has found the Practicum to be particularly beneficial as a "friendly forum in which to share ideas and to talk about things that would just stay there!"

Many stories get shared in these group settings. Another superintendent initiate confesses that he still pinches himself sometimes to see if he is real. His having landed one of the most prestigious districts in the state continues to shock him. Also strange is the fact that his predecessor left to become superintendent in a neighboring district, a district that is currently involved in a legal battle with his!

Like all new superintendents, those in CH's group talk constantly about superintendent-board relations and problem employees. Sometimes, the issues that superintendents face in small districts surprise those who lead large ones. A board member's desire to select a grass cutter for the district is not one that usually troubles a superintendent in a medium- to large-sized district. Yet, micromanagement by board members and their meddling in personnel matters are common issues, despite the size of the district.

Creating a culture for change is another issue of major interest to group members. With the tenure of a superintendent so short, teachers often adopt a "this too shall pass" attitude that prevents a major stumbling block to school improvement efforts of the new superintendent. Ways to gain the commitment of teachers is a topic of interest to all new superintendents.

CH's group members are delighted to discover that they are not alone, that their issues and problems are similar to those of most other new superintendents. They also like the reassurance they receive from the group that they were doing an "Okay" job, and that they enjoy sharing information and ideas with one another.

Another Look at the Practicum

NM is recently retired from a superintendency in southern New Jersey. He spent 17 years in the same district, one that was medium-sized and fairly diverse, without a lot of money to spend on education. NM has an earned doctorate from Glassboro State College and is an avid reader and active learner. NM has been nicknamed the "Practicum Pied Piper" because of his success in attracting new superintendents to his groups. At one time, he had two groups of seven each going at the same time.

NM's new superintendents generally come from small, rural, and less affluent districts, largely K–8. In these districts, the superintendent must be a "jack of all trades" because he or she has only a few support staff to help. Oftentimes, small, rural districts are forced to select inexperienced administrators, due to the comparatively low salaries they feel they can offer. These superintendents generally face a steep learning curve and limited financial resources with which to work. For example, one of NM's new superintendents rose to the job from the position of elementary principal and, in addition to learning the myriad of central office job functions, in his first year found himself planning and marketing a building program and, in his second year, overseeing the construction of a new school.

Perhaps, in part, because they share the same challenges, NM's groups form especially strong bonds, and their professional relationships continue beyond the experience of the Practicum. One recently told me that he frequently talks to other group members a year after the group ended, and that he often receives great leads from them when he advertises a position in the paper. Others from small districts have begun to share services and personnel to reduce costs and improve quality.

Since the groups are formed regionally rather than by county, members find the opportunity to meet with administrators from other parts of the state to be especially rewarding. They also find that "breaking bread" together provides a positive atmosphere for group meetings. Most meetings are held as either breakfast or dinner sessions.

NM starts his first meeting by having each person share some of his or her background, some success stories, and a few reasons for becoming a school administrator. He enforces the rules: All conversations are strictly confidential. Open, truthful communications are the norm. No one dominates, and all participate at a level that is personally comfortable to them.

Group meetings provide each initiate with an opportunity to share a "right now" problem, and to receive feedback from the other new superintendents and from NM. Others ask for further information, they ask questions, and they offer suggestions or give examples from their own experiences. No one judges or evaluates the decisions made by others. They are simply there to listen and to help.

An example of a challenging problem faced by one of NM's group members was the demand from her board of education, early in her first year, to "get rid of" a tenured administrator. NM sensed that her board was putting her to the test and trying to determine who would control personnel decisions, the superintendent, or the board! This sticky issue transcended the entire year of the Practicum as it ran its course, and through monthly analysis and discussion became a learning situation for all members. The owner of the problem received practical help and enormous emotional support from others as she worked through the legal, ethical, and practical aspects of this problem. NM was able to mentor her between meetings through phone calls and e-mail and, at one time, actually made an instant visit to her district to help her prepare for a board meeting that promised to be very difficult for her.

Not every new superintendent is equally comfortable discussing problems with the whole group, but each learns from the process. Those who are reticent inevitably find one or two others to confide in; often, but not always, it is NM. Their discussions take place by e-mail, telephone, before the meeting, and in the parking lot while the group is leaving.

As is true with each of the four Practicum Leaders, NM has grown from the experience of leading groups and mentoring new superintendents. He admits that the Practicum has improved his listening skills, and that helping others has provided him with an enormous amount of personal satisfaction. In addition to personal support, NM provides the group members with technical information and resources to help them grow and learn. In his 30+ years in the business, there is not much that NM has not learned about the superintendency. He shares work samples, such as policies, newsletters, books, and current research of interest to the group. NM finds that the three major challenges that constantly surface from new superintendents are board-superintendent relations, communicating with the board, and handling difficult personnel situations.

An almost unanimous complaint of new superintendents is . . . I have no time to myself. This job is all-consuming! This is a complaint that tends to fall on deaf ears. Spouses generally perceive their superintendent partner as a workaholic who needs to manage his or her time better. Board members view the superintendent as a servant who must always be at their beck and call. Teachers say, "You wanted the job, so don't complain!" Community members feel the pay justifies the time. Practicum participants find it helpful to have a empathetic ear once in a while, and that ear is found within the group.

Evaluating the Practicum for New Superintendents

Staying power, both in the job and in the district, is the best indicator of the Practicum's success. Having just completed three years, it is still too early to determine the long-time effects of the program. However, given an average tenure of three years in the same job for all superintendents, one can assume that new superintendents might suffer greater turnover than experienced ones, due to their lack of experience.

At the close of the 2001–2002 academic year, out of 50 new superintendents who had been served in the program, only four were no longer in the same job. Three of these had retired, and one left her district by mutual consent with her board and was immediately hired as assistant superintendent by a prominent New Jersey district. One of the three retirees had suffered difficulties on the job with a particularly difficult board member. The other two had become superintendents near the end of their careers and, when they became eligible to retire, chose to do so absent of any pressure from their boards.

The IELRR at Seton Hall University will continue to track the success (and failure) rates of individual participants as the program continues. Satisfaction of the program participants is another valid and reliable way to measure its success. I regularly talk to the Practicum Leaders and periodically interview select participants to assess this factor. The responses are all favorable and, in fact, call for a second year of the program. Many have expressed interest in holding regular, but perhaps fewer, meetings during the second year to continue sharing and solving problems together.

Since the Practicum now serves approximately one half of all new superintendents in New Jersey, it provides an opportunity to design an assessment that includes a "control group." This project will be explored with local universities during the next year, in the hope that a doctoral dissertation student will recognize the opportunity presented by our unique data.

Starting Your Own Program

The Practicum for New Superintendents is a simple, yet rich model that can easily be reproduced by any organization that is interested in adding to the success of new superintendents. Following is a series of steps that are recommended, based on the practical knowledge gained by doing it!

1. Assess the market . . . find out how many first-time superintendents are in your state.
2. Assess the need . . . are their any other programs or services being provided to first time superintendents by other organizations?
3. Design the program . . . use this model or modify it as you feel necessary.
4. Create marketing materials . . . Web sites, brochures, advertisements, letters, public presentations, and so forth.
5. Budget the program . . . expenses include stipends for leaders and mentors and organizational overhead.
6. Seek financial assistance . . . grants are extremely helpful in building the program.
7. Select leaders and mentors . . . make sure you pick good listeners and facilitators, as well as highly successful current, or former, superintendents.
8. Train leaders and mentors . . . ensure consistency, while also allowing for creativity.
9. Recruit new superintendents . . . use your marketing materials and personal contacts.
10. Launch the program . . . start as soon as you have a sufficient number (no less than three; no more than ten).
11. Monitor and support the group(s) . . . stay in touch with the leader or mentor; hold leader and mentor meetings periodically to share ideas and group problem solve.
12. Evaluate the program . . . use ideas in this book and/or others to evaluate your successes.
13. Celebrate your success . . . hold periodic reunions, write journal articles, do presentations, and spread the word.

Companion Program for Aspiring Superintendents

The Practicum is one of two leadership programs designed to attract and support new superintendents in New Jersey. The first program, the New Superintendent's Initiative (NSI), was started in 1998 to inspire and support talented aspiring superintendents, especially minorities and females, in meeting their career goals.

NSI provides one year of executive leadership training, individually tailored to the participants' strengths and deficiencies, through a personal mentor, and four weekend training sessions. Each candidate, who is selected through a highly competitive process, is matched with a "personal trainer" for one year of formal apprenticeship. During that time, they work together to design an individual leadership plan and work collectively to explore current and practical leadership issues. Considerable attention is given to the process of applying for jobs, including taped interviews and critiques.

The success of the first 18 graduates has been impressive. Eleven (11) graduates are now serving as superintendents in New Jersey. Six (6) of the 11 graduates are female, three of whom are African-Americans employed by predominantly white, suburban districts. Four other graduates have received significant promotional positions, and the remaining three graduates are active in searches at this time.

Conclusion

The need for continuing and expanded efforts to recruit, train, and support principals and superintendents is obvious. If public education is to improve in the ways that the American public now insists, schools and districts require highly competent and committed leaders.

Mentoring is a timeless and proven method for developing skills and values in protégés, dating back to the Ancient Greek civilization. Mentor-mentee relationships among educators have been in effect for years on an informal basis, and will continue. However, by formalizing mentoring into programs designed specifically to prepare and support new leaders, it can be put to greater use and generate greater impact.

We believe that the Practicum improves leadership skills. Leadership is all about relationships. I was once given a T-shirt, in jest, with the statement, "I am the leader, which way did they go?" Getting everyone onboard and marching in the same direction is the primary challenge of a leader. Superintendents regularly deal with trustees with special interests, staff members with entrenched ideas, and unions with their own agenda. They work with parents who focus narrowly on their children and taxpayers who care only about their pocketbooks. How to convince these constituents to abandon their selfish perspectives for the greater good is a primary topic of group meetings. To the extent that new superintendents hone their skills in this dimension as a result of the Practicum, this program is improving tomorrow's leaders.

References

Daresh, J. (2001). *Leaders helping leaders*. Thousand Oaks, CA: Corwin Press.

For Consideration

1. How can the consultation model, explained in this chapter, be used in any mentoring relationship?

2. Why should mentoring be formalized? How should experienced teachers and administrators work to transform their own school's mentoring into a formalized structure?

3. How do the mentoring partnerships, described in this chapter, work to create learning?

Chapter 9

Strategies to Sustain a Mentoring Culture

Henry Kiernan

"Those who have torches will pass them on to others."
—Plato

Introduction

Before Homer's Odysseus left on his long journey, he directed the education and upbringing of his son to his friend, Mentor. Almost 2,500 years later, entrusting the development of a new teacher has gained renewed focus as America's schools face an increasing need to hire new teachers. The stark reality of hiring over 2 million new teachers needed before the end of this first decade of the 21st century is just the first challenge. The next problem is that close to one half of new teachers leave the classroom within their first five years of teaching. Schools simply have to change the way they are recruiting, hiring, and retaining teachers.

Many states are addressing these concerns by revising teacher licensure requirements and by recommending, if not requiring, school districts to implement mentoring programs. For example, New Jersey requires that all first-year teachers receive an in-school mentoring program. Yet, as with most state mandates, the process to implement effective mentoring programs did not transfer into training and support for school districts to establish effective practices.

What Is Mentoring?

The best way to define mentoring is by first defining what it is not. Mentoring is not a short-term "buddy system," whereby the new teacher has a buddy who demonstrates how to report attendance or where to find classroom supplies. Nor is it a one-day school building orientation, whereby school administrators demonstrate to new teachers how to conduct a fire drill. While these tasks are necessary, they do not reflect the long-term needs of new teachers. Instead, mentoring is a collaborative professional relationship between an experienced teacher and a new teacher that provides time for both to inquire and reflect about teaching practice and student learning. It involves both the mentor and the new teacher, or protégé, having the time to observe teaching in each other's classes and in other teachers' classes over a period of time. Thus, it is a long-term reciprocal process of reflection, dialogue, practice, and commitment to learning.

The mentor as "midwife to our dreams"

Bruno Bettleheim, in *The Uses of Enchantment,* refers to mentors as the midwives to our dreams. The analogy of the midwife is an interesting one, as it lies at the heart of the mentor's goal of encouraging responsibility within the protégé. Moving the new teacher or administrator toward developing independence, making good judgments, and possessing resilience are the true goals of a successful mentor. A mentor assists the protégé with skills to help him or her achieve his or her dreams.

Since the early Greeks demonstrated the need for mentors, mentors today come in many different forms. The most basic are the mentor who offers information and technical expertise, the mentor who can help interpret the norms and culture, and the mentor who serves as the role model. Mentors assume a variety of roles: teacher, coach, role model, guide, advocate, confidant, nurturer, learner, consultant, and sponsor, to name a few. From all the literature on the basic assumptions and beliefs about mentors, it seems that the critical determiner of a successful mentor-protégé relationship is candor. There must be mutual respect and trust, and as we know from life experience, the building of a level of trust takes time and effort. Yet, the importance of trust-building in the mentoring experience is often understated. Even more understated is the leadership ability of a successful mentor in imparting the culture of a school to a protégé. Roland Barth (2001) believes that what lies at the heart of what it means to be a professional is when teachers "take the helm," or take the leadership to improve the school. He notes in an essay that appeared in *Education Week*:

> "More than anything else, it is the culture of the school that determines the achievement of teacher and student alike."

What are some qualities to look for in mentors?

First, and above all, a good mentor knows that listening is more productive than talking. Too often, the mentor's role becomes one of "the sage on the front stage" rather than the "guide on the side." There clearly are appropriate times for the mentor to do the talking, and there are far more appropriate times for the mentor to listen, ask questions, and seek potential solutions from the new teacher or administrator. It is always a matter of balancing the degree of sharing knowledge and expertise and the prospect of helping the protégé seek a solution. It is also quite possible that the solution a protégé implements may end in failure. A good mentor knows that it is wise to provide the protégé the freedom to experiment, as well as to share his or her own failures and successes. The focus needs to be on what was learned.

Learning to listen and learning when to talk require perspective. The mentor must be able to encourage responsibility and communicate the belief that learning is a lifetime pursuit. As our best athletes continue to seek new knowledge from coaches, we need to develop a culture within schools that promotes the belief that new and veteran teachers and administrators must continue to learn from each other.

Mentors also need to possess a strong dose of self-esteem, as they need to realize that they should expect nothing in return for their services. While some school districts provide a monetary stipend to the mentor, this is in no way commensurate with the time, effort, and dedication a good mentor provides. A mentor has to understand that the very act of providing guidance to the protégé does not necessarily translate into satisfaction. The most visible gratification for the mentor comes from the ability to watch the protégé develop and grow professionally over time. Yet those who have mentored know that the process of mentoring provides more. By working in partnership with new teachers, mentors enjoy reflecting on their own personal growth as teachers, as well as continued, ongoing learning about the craft of teaching.

However, the real challenge for a good mentor is to find the balance between offering supportive guidance and critique. One strategy that works well is to provide mentors with some professional development training or retraining in the use of peer coaching. Peer-coaching strategies employ several questioning techniques that help a mentor guide the protégé toward reflecting about a lesson before hearing comments from the mentor's observations. This process of self-assessment should always occur before the mentor's critique. Beth Tatum & Patti McWhorter, in *Teacher Mentor: A Dialogue for Collaborative Learning* (1999), stress the importance of this self-assessment or reflection as a way to develop trust between the mentor and the protégé. Their own experiences in working with new teachers that it is necessary for mentors to provide early intervention and support and have shown that teacher candidates ". . . are resilient, for the most part, and respect honesty from their mentor teachers when it is accompanied by visible support" (p. 31).

What qualities should a good protégé possess?

A good protégé has to be open to learning from the mentor. The mentor and the protégé are not equal partners. This seems obvious, however, if this openness does not manifest itself within the protégé, then a road map for frustration will quickly begin. Negotiation is a wiser path than confrontation.

Just as a good mentor needs to listen, so does a good protégé. Being able to ask the right questions is a skill in itself, and a protégé needs to be able to speak frankly with the mentor. This also takes some time, so a good protégé needs to be blessed with ample patience and flexibility.

A good protégé also needs to be a good observer. The best opportunity is for the protégé to watch the mentor teach. This should also include time for the protégé to observe other teachers as well. It is also necessary for the protégé to understand that not everything observed will be met without judgment.

Just as a good mentor realizes that learning is ongoing, so, too, does a good protégé realize that becoming a good teacher or school administrator will be a lifelong process. And the best way to learn is to keep a journal, log, or professional portfolio. The process of reflection is a good way to make sense of thoughts, events, and ideas.

What is the best way to choose a mentor?

School districts will need to address this question, based upon their own resources and conditions. Ideally, it would be best to find a mentor with content knowledge in the same field as the new teacher. However, that may be impossible for some schools. One way to provide some content expertise is to consider long-distance mentors by way of a professional organization, or within other schools in a district or neighboring districts, while at the same time maintaining a mentor in the local school who can provide pedagogical expertise. While there is much excitement about long-distance mentoring by way of electronic means, there are special challenges, such as the lack of a personal connection to provide the everyday contact that most new teachers need.

Other considerations may involve both cross-cultural and gender differences, as well as generational differences that can be found between matching mentors and protégés. A recent newspaper editorial reflected on how baby boomers, the "Don't Trust Anyone Under 30" generation, struggle with their new role as mentors for the Generation X-ers, who only know the youth culture and have trouble trusting elders.

Yet, the most difficult task for a school district is to assist the mentor in understanding the role. It is critically important to conduct training for potential mentors. This is not something that "just happens" because the mentor assigned is noted for expert teaching or administrative skills. While there are certain qualities that make a good mentor, the carrying out of the tasks involved is something that needs reflection and guidance. No school district should assume that a mentoring program should survive on the good will of well-skilled teachers who volunteer to serve as mentors. Potential mentors must be trained on the best strategies, to transfer the norms and expectations of the school's culture.

One successful strategy is for a school district to develop its own mentoring guide and to use experienced mentors to "turn key" train potential mentors. This training should be accomplished before the new school year begins, so that the mentor can meet the protégé before school opening. Some topics for the training can include: (1) strategies for the mentor to collaborate with the protégé, such as teaching a lesson and/or planning a unit together; (2) strategies to ask coaching questions; and (3) strategies to model reflection.

Mentoring Benefits

Little research exists to support best practices in mentoring. While there are certainly several researched studies on the needs of teacher candidates and student teachers, less is known about the ever-changing needs of new teachers during their first, second, and third years of teaching. Even less is known about the needs of experienced teachers who change schools as they deal with a new environment and culture. As for school administrators, it is rare to find schools that assign mentors. In most cases, a new principal is left to sort through the culture of the school and to learn it quickly. It is even more critical for a superintendent to learn the culture, as self-mentoring for new school administrators, particularly for chief school administrators, is generally the rule.

As the trend exists for more people to change jobs, choose new careers, or find new paths, one of the first lessons for any new candidate in a new job is to learn the culture of the institution. This immersion into a new culture is often mentioned in the case studies that appear in this book as new teachers and administrators experience new ways of doing things, some of which will require transitioning to understanding new procedures, policies, and how the system works. An effective mentoring program that facilitates learning to adapt to the new culture should ameliorate the transition for new employees.

Whatever the context and nature of a school's mentoring program, there are many studies in the field that prove that positive mentoring experiences increase job satisfaction, productivity, and employee retention. For example, Gold (1999) found, in a study of new teachers in New Jersey, that the attrition rate of teachers who experienced mentoring in their induction program was 5%, compared to an 18% attrition rate for new teachers trained in traditional college programs without mentoring. Evertson & Smithey (2000) concluded that novice teachers who worked with trained mentors possessed a higher level of instructional skills than new teachers whose mentors were not trained.

Yet, there are also cases where mentoring programs fail as a result of bad matching between the mentor and the protégé, weak follow-up experiences, and lack of support from school leaders. In order to avoid failure, a school district needs to monitor and evaluate the progress of its mentoring program by conducting ongoing dialogue with mentors, to assess strengths and weaknesses and to reinforce the roles and responsibilities of mentors. In addition, a school district needs to invest in providing time for the mentor and protégé to reflect on learning.

How does a successful mentoring program promote and sustain a professional culture?

It is the responsibility of a school to design a mentoring program that first "trains the trainer," assuring that mentors possess the skills, qualities, and abilities necessary to meet the needs of new teachers and administrators. This is not an easy task, as new teachers are now entering the profession from nontraditional ways. Rather than a traditional student-teaching experience, many states have developed alternative routes to teaching that do not offer student-teaching experiences. In New Jersey, the alternate route to receiving a teaching license allows a candidate, who has achieved a bachelor's degree and an approved Praxis test score, to be employed by a school district without any educational course work at either the undergraduate or graduate level. Instead, teachers can be hired to begin teaching and then may choose to attend evening classes to learn about pedagogy after spending a day teaching in the classroom. This alternate-route approach has both been lauded as a way to find candidates to fill positions during a teacher shortage and criticized by those who are skeptical of a "learn by doing" approach. Certainly, it may take more time to instill the values of a school culture if new teachers are overstretched by attending evening classes.

The many benefits of a well-designed mentoring program are evidenced in the case studies found in this book. From preservice teachers, to teachers, and to superintendents, there is one common ingredient—reflection.

There is enough evidence to suggest that one of the best strategies for adult learners to retain their new knowledge is to consciously reflect on their learning. Lois J. Zachary, in *The Mentor's Guide* (2000), defines the process of reflection as "an introspective dialogue carried on in written form that stimulates the raising of questions, provokes the assessment of learning, and enables the integration of new learning" (p. xx). By encouraging new teachers to write down their reflections, mentors enable them to promote conversation by helping new teachers to capture classroom events and to organize their thoughts. By writing to reflect on a classroom activity, a protégé is able to set the stage for a dialogue with a mentor. Some very good strategies to begin this dialogue can be found in *Mentoring Beginning Teachers* (Boreen, Johnson, Niday, & Potts, 2000, pp. 67–84).

As a school, or any institution, searches for the best design to implement a mentoring program, the reflections from these model programs demonstrate the many lessons learned by all involved, sprinkled with the knowledge that comes from experience and expertise. Yet, the most difficult work that comes from implementation is how to sustain a successful mentoring program that will continually reap benefits for both mentors and protégés, and for the institutions they serve. The key to sustaining a successful mentoring program is to make mentoring the cornerstone of a district's supervision and evaluation system that is linked to student achievement. When professional development, mentoring, curriculum development, school, and district goals are aligned with a district's supervision-evaluation system, then the school culture changes to ensure that mentoring new teachers receives the highest priority.

How can a successful mentoring program be implemented? Where can a school find the time and resources to foster a successful mentoring program?

Whenever I present on the topic of mentoring at state and national conferences, the first question from the audience goes something like this: "We don't have enough time in our school day to create a mentoring program such as the one you describe. How can we do it?" The usual restraints include time for mentors and protégés to meet, time for administrators to work with new teachers, and a lack of time for follow-up meetings between mentors and protégés. Given the current structure of most schools, it does seem like a daunting task. With so much time spent on classroom observations of new teachers, administrators hardly have the time to oversee an effective mentoring program. Administrators spend so much time in conducting mandated classroom observations of tenured teachers that new teachers, who need the guidance and support, struggle along waiting for their turn to be observed. There needs to be a differentiation between new teachers engaged in a mentoring program, as compared to experienced teachers who are routinely observed by local or state mandate.

While each school district may have unique contractual obligations, evaluation should be separate from mentoring. In fact, a mentor assigned to a teacher should not be responsible for writing an evaluation of a classroom observation. The mentor's role of advocacy for the protégé would be jeopardized under such a system. At the same time, a good mentor needs to have established trust with the protégé so that weaknesses can be identified quickly and corrected. Yet, the irony rests in the fact that no other profession makes the same demands on protégés as it does mentors. New teachers are held to the same standard of evaluation, and in most cases, the same procedures that employ hierarchical one-way communication, as experienced teachers. No one expects a new architect to design single-handedly a new skyscraper, yet a new teacher is expected to be judged on the same checklist of skills as a highly experienced teacher.

The major problem rests in the fact that the current system of observation and evaluation of all teachers is flawed. While very few school districts make any distinction between experienced and new teachers, even fewer school districts develop shared assumptions and values about good teaching. There needs to be a differentiated evaluation system that allows for new teachers who succeed in a trusting mentoring program to continue to grow beyond the first year of teaching. Why not infuse the same principles, values, and outcomes of a successful mentoring program, such as reflective dialogue, professional research on student achievement, and nurturing trust within and across the school culture? The process of implementing an effective mentoring program can be developed at the same time by taking a hard look at revising a district's evaluation and supervision system. It is a logical step in changing the culture of a school. Such a change will place with the teaching and learning process, and the goal of student achievement, as the foundation of educational decision making in a school.

At West Morris Regional, we began this process seven years ago, when Tom McGreal, Professor Emeritus at the University of Illinois at Urbana—Champaign, spent a summer day with our school administrators, discussing ways to revise our evaluation and supervision procedures. We had read Charlotte Danielson's research (2000) on effective teaching practice and began working with teachers to draft our own descriptors of effective teaching.

I vividly recall how, after a full day of discussing the latest research in the field of supervision and evaluation, agreeing for the need for change, and establishing some differentiated supervision models, we then showed Professor McGreal our model form to use when conducting a classroom observation. Professor McGreal studied it closely, and there was a long, silent pause. He then held it up in front of us and crumpled it and threw it in the nearby waste bin. Needless to say, the dramatic move caught us by surprise. He looked up at us and stated: "You have now developed a strong sense of what needs to be done philosophically and have a good set of research tools to support your efforts. This observation sheet, containing a checklist of boxes denoting categories of superior, effective and needs improvement, does not advance your cause." He was right, of course, and we realized it would take another school year of discussion before we could move toward change. That extra year bought us the time to implement a successful change effort. We established a committee of teachers, administrators, and one Board member that was cochaired by a teacher and an administrator. The committee helped draft descriptors of effective teaching for teachers and other professionals, reviewed our Board policy revision, and created the forms that would best match our mentoring program with our evaluation system.

It was critical to make this a grassroots reform effort, and so, the committee's work was of interest to the administration, Board of Education, and the school community. It was also important to involve the Board of Education from the beginning, since it was necessary to change Board policy. The previous policy referred to the accountability measures found in a nondifferentiated rating system for teachers, and the new policy (Figure 1) sets up a clear expectation of the district's commitment to excellence in teaching and learning. Consequently, the new policy supports a professional assessment system that is based on rigorous teaching standards and comprehensive differentiated professional growth opportunities. The district believes that:

- Assessment of performance is designed to promote excellence in teaching and learning.
- Assessment is a dynamic, ongoing process that requires review and revision, based on evolving research, practices, and experiences of the West Morris Regional High School District.
- Professionals grow and learn in different ways. Committed teachers develop their professional capabilities over time and, often, are at different stages of development necessitating a differentiated system of assessment.
- Mutual trust and respect are the cornerstones of a professional learning community.

The next step in the process to reform our evaluation system was to seek a waiver from the State Department of Education. New Jersey, as with most states, requires that all tenured teachers receive a minimum of two classroom observations per school year. We, therefore, sought and secured a waiver to implement our new system that would allow administrators more time to work with new and nontenured teachers.

With the adoption of the new Board policy, the committee then moved toward completing the Descriptors of Effective Teaching (Figure 2). Furthermore, the committee defined each descriptor so that teachers and administrators would have a clear understanding of what each descriptor meant (Figure 3). It is not recommended that any district just "cut and paste" their own list of descriptors. Teachers, administrators, and policymakers need to work together to agree to those descriptors that they mutually believe represent the best teaching to meet the needs of their community's students.

Figure 1. West Morris Regional High School District Professional Supervision and Evaluation System

Policy

The Board of Education recognizes the importance of professional growth, based on reflective practice and trusts in, and expects, a high level of competency from its teaching staff. Mutual trust and respect are cornerstones of a professional environment, in which staff and students engage in a continuous learning process. Inherent in an effective supervision-evaluation system is the belief that professional development is ongoing, self-directed, and dynamic.

The Board acknowledges that assessment of professional staff is a dynamic process that must consider both formative and summative perspectives. It is the belief of the Board that any assessment system requires yearly review and revision, based on evolving research, analysis, and experiences of the West Morris Regional High School District to remain vital to the needs of the professional staff and continue to promote student learning.

Recognizing that adults learn in different ways and in different stages, the Board supports a differentiated system of supervision. This system shall provide for a continuum of learning and growth opportunities. It shall further recognize that the needs of new and inexperienced staff are different from those of more experienced staff. Finally, it shall recognize that individuals may, from time to time, require special assistance and intervention.

Formative assessment promotes professional growth, improves the instructional process, and affects the academic achievement of students. It involves an ongoing dialogue between professional partners that encourages collegiality. This process supports creative and diverse pedagogy. It is intended to result in reflection and purposeful action by all members of the learning community.

Summative assessment considers the progress of a staff member toward meeting professional competencies. Formal and informal observations, professional improvement plans, activities, and professional growth efforts can be used to determine overall performance.

Figure 2. Descriptors of Effective Teaching

Fundamental Competencies

The Descriptors of Effective Teaching represent those professional standards that each staff member should possess, or be striving to attain, in the quest for professional excellence. At the same time, the district acknowledges that excellence requires a strong foundation of fundamental competencies that tenured staff must demonstrate consistently.

The teacher:
- demonstrates content knowledge
- designs written plans that reflect goals and objectives of the curriculum
- evaluates outcomes of instruction for the achievement of stated goals
- communicates assessment criteria and standards are clear
- fosters a code of mutual respect and models respectful behavior
- manages instructional time efficiently

cont.

> - monitors student standards of conduct
> - articulates directions clearly
> - creates procedures that are clear and consistent
> - provides effective feedback in a timely manner
> - oversees and maintains direction of the lesson
> - adheres to school and district procedures and deadlines
> - communicates with families about the instructional program and individual students
> - demonstrates a commitment to the continuing development of teaching skills and lifelong learning
> - actively participates in self-directed professional development pathway

Descriptors of Effective Teaching

The West Morris Regional High School District acknowledges the importance of describing the knowledge, skills, and accomplishments that comprise effective teaching. It agrees with the National Board for Professional Teaching Standards that high and rigorous standards should serve as a framework for ongoing growth in teaching expertise that ultimately results in increased student learning. The Descriptors of Effective Teaching represent those professional standards that each staff member should possess, or be striving to attain, in the quest for professional excellence. The district also recognizes that excellence requires a strong foundation of fundamental skills that members of the district's professional staff must demonstrate consistently.

Planning and Preparation

The teacher demonstrates content knowledge:
- demonstrates knowledge and experience beyond textbook
- uses materials that reflect current and relevant research
- connects present lessons to past lessons
- relates content to other disciplines
- uses a variety of resources for teaching and learning
- updates planning and collection of materials

The teacher designs written plans that reflect goals and objectives of the curriculum:
- delineates expectations for short- and long-term assignments
- uses varied instructional groups as appropriate to different instructional goals
- provides a variety of support materials to enhance content including, but not limited to: text, articles, handouts, audio and videotapes, Web sites and software to enhance goals, objectives, content

- articulates relationship between materials (text, articles, handouts, audio and videotapes, Web sites and software) to the content of curriculum
- uses materials that provide opportunity for application

The teacher frequently evaluates outcomes of instruction for the achievement of stated goals:
- communicates assessment criteria and standards to students
- varies type of assessment techniques
- reviews results of testing to confirm understanding of concept and reteaches when necessary

The teacher knows about, chooses from, and implements appropriate strategies to teaching:
- displays understanding of different approaches to knowledge
- has knowledge of student interests
- displays knowledge of student's skills and knowledge for each student, including those with special needs

Classroom Environment

The teacher establishes a culture for learning:
- conveys the expectation that all students will achieve at high levels of learning
- relates the relevancy of concepts to life experiences and usefulness
- creates an environment in which students work together and take responsibility for learning
- encourages students to seek help to support their learning

The teacher fosters a code of mutual respect and models respectful behavior:
- interacts positively with students in ways that validate student contributions
- recognizes accomplishments and the process students use to demonstrate understanding

The teacher manages instructional time efficiently:
- manages classroom procedures
- has materials, aids, and facility ready for use
- creates smooth transitions

The teacher manages student standards of conduct:
- conveys standards of conduct to all students
- ensures that standards of conduct are clear to all students
- monitors student behavior
- responds appropriately and respects the students' dignity

Instruction

The teacher communicates to students clearly and accurately:
- develops and distributes requirements, expectations, and assessment criteria in the context of the overall course framework and syllabus
- communicates focus for unit and daily lessons
- articulates directions
- develops clear and consistent procedures

The teacher uses a variety of questioning and discussion techniques:
- accepts and encourages divergent thinking
- incorporates higher-order thinking skills
- encourages students to be creative, analytical, and self-evaluative

The teacher engages students in learning:
- acknowledges and accommodates for different levels of ability
- provides tasks appropriate to level
- provides opportunity for application of concepts
- uses a variety of teaching activities
- maintains focus of instruction

The teacher provides meaningful feedback to students:
- provides frequent feedback, assessment of students, and reteaching
- uses a variety of evaluation activities
- provides effective feedback in a timely manner

Professional Responsibilities

The teacher articulates principal goals of instructional practice which promote student learning:
- articulates strategies used to accomplish goals and evaluates the effectiveness of those strategies
- demonstrates self-awareness of strengths and pedagogical methods

The teacher adheres to school and district procedures and deadlines:
- documents student progress
- maintains accurate records
- meets deadlines
- performs school duties diligently

The teacher communicates with families about the instructional program and individual students:
- provides information to parents as appropriate about the instructional program
- communicates with parents about students' lack of progress and is available to respond to parental concerns

The teacher actively demonstrates concern for the schoolwide community:
- participates in school and district projects
- supports and cooperates with colleagues
- participates in team or departmental decision making
- implements subject area building and/or district initiatives

The teacher demonstrates a commitment to the continuing development of teaching skills and lifelong learning:
- participates in self-directed professional development pathway
- participates in professional development activities (conferences, workshops, seminars)
- integrates professional growth and interest into school and classroom environment
- presents and facilitates learning activities for colleagues

The committee also recognized that Descriptors of Effective Teaching did not affect the work responsibilities of all professionals who work in a school. For example, guidance counselors, nurses, and librarians also needed to be included in this reform effort both for mentoring and supervision and for evaluation purposes. Thus, the committee worked with these professionals to design descriptors that were directly applied to their job responsibilities. These descriptors can be found in the appendix at the end of this chapter.

With a new policy and descriptors of effective teaching in place, the committee next prepared the development of three supervision-evaluation pathways that would recognize differentiation and the varied needs toward moving all teachers into the second pathway or the self-directed professional pathway. Much of our work was developed in consultation with Professor McGreal, who coauthored with Charlotte Danielson, *Teacher Evaluation To Enhance Professional Practice*. Their work was published during the first year of our implementation of our new mentoring program and supervision and evaluation system. An overview of each pathway is found in Figure 3. The Appendix provides sample forms for classroom observation, the interim report, the professional development portfolio, and the annual evaluation summary report.

In the first pathway, the directive supervision evaluation pathway, all new teachers are placed. Whether a teacher is new to the profession or an experienced teacher new to the district, this pathway provides the recognition that the staff members placed in this first pathway need a mentor and also administrative support in order to reach the second pathway. Teachers in the first pathway receive a minimum of five 60-minute classroom observations, of which at least one observation follows the same class of students for at least two consecutive lessons.

Figure 3. Leading to Three Levels of Development

I. Directive Supervision Evaluation Pathway	II. Self-Directed Professional Growth Pathway	III. Professional Assistance Pathway
Participants: • New, inexperienced teachers • New, experienced teachers	**Participants:** • Tenured teachers who are demonstrating competency in the Descriptors of Effective Teaching	**Participants:** • Teachers in need of specific professional assistance in identified area(s) of the Descriptors of Effective Teaching
Purpose: • To ensure that the Descriptors of Effective Teaching are understood, accepted, and demonstrated. • To provide support in implementing the Descriptors of Effective Teaching • To provide accountability for decisions to continue employment	**Purpose:** • To enhance professional growth • To create opportunity for professional dialogue • To focus on accomplishment of subject area, school, and district initiatives	**Purpose:** • To enable a tenured teacher the opportunity to seek assistance in any descriptor • To provide a more structured process for a tenured teacher who may benefit from more support • To provide due process for disciplinary action
Procedure: • Formal and informal observations • Professional Development Portfolio • New Teacher Training • Mentoring	**Procedure:** • Continuous informal assessment • Development and implementation of the Professional Growth Plan	**Procedure:** • Awareness Phase • Assistance Plan
Method: • Classroom observation with feedback • Participation in portfolio process • Participation in required professional training sessions • Dialogue and meetings with mentor • Peer Coaching • Annual Evaluation Summary Report	**Method:** • Ongoing informal observation and discussion of teacher performance • Collaborative development of individual or team Professional Growth Plans • Dialogue among teachers and teams and administrators • Reflection and summary of process • Annual Evaluation Summary Report	**Method:** • Conferences • Formal and informal observation • Development and implementation of a Professional Assistance Plan • Annual Evaluation Summary Report

Direct Supervision Evaluation Pathway

This pathway provides a directive and structured system for nontenured teachers to meet professional teaching standards that are defined in the district's Descriptors of Effective Teaching. Both summative and formative assessment approaches are used to develop the knowledge and skills base that constitute excellence in teaching. These include:

Observation

The purpose of observation is to gather data on classroom practice as it relates to the professional teaching standards and provide structured feedback and suggestions on performance. Nontenured teachers will be observed a minimum of three to five full class periods per year. All first-year teachers will be observed formally four times and informally once. Second-year teachers will be observed formally three to four times and informally once. Third-year teachers will be formally observed at least three times. For the first-year teacher, at least one of these observations will be of two to three days in duration within the same class period. The principal or his or her designee and the Director of Staff Development will conduct these observations. Pre- and postconference will be held for each formal observation. Specific feedback on Descriptors of Effective Teaching, particularly the fundamental teaching competencies, will be discussed and recorded after each postconference. Ongoing verbal feedback is also critical to this process. Commencing in September, nontenured teachers will be observed approximately every six weeks, with completion no later than the end of April.

Mentoring

The purpose of mentoring is to provide a supportive learning environment, in which new teachers can gain confidence in instructional competencies, increase professional knowledge, and learn the culture of the school and district. A mentor will be assigned to all new (experienced and inexperienced) staff members by September 1st. The district mentoring program guidelines will provide direction for this one-year partnership. Mentor–new-teacher relationships will be collegial in nature and activities will include, but not be limited to. orientation, consultation, and peer-coaching experiences.

New-Teacher Training

The purpose of new-teacher training is to provide opportunities to acquire and/or refine new skills and knowledge related to district professional teaching standards. New, inexperienced teachers will attend 15 hours, and new, experienced teachers five hours of district-designed professional development that focuses on topics related to fundamental competencies. The initial training session will be held during the summer, with subsequent sessions scheduled during the school year.

Professional Development Portfolio/Professional Growth Plan

The purpose of the professional development portfolio is to increase competency in the Descriptors of Effective Teaching. First-year teachers will focus on the development of a planning process, including the creation of a planning binder that will guide classroom instruction. Inexperienced second-year teachers will identify a learning focus that connects to Descriptors of Effective Teaching. At the discretion of the administration, second-year experienced teachers will either complete a portfolio or participate in the professional growth plan process. Teachers will develop learning plans, select portfolio partners to meet with informally, engage in learning activities, collect artifacts, attend formal portfolio meetings, and record reflections about their professional growth and connections to student learning. The administrator will meet with teachers mid-year and, by the end of April, develop a collaborative summary of progress toward meeting learning goals, including activities, reflection on learning, and determination of future direction and goals. All third-year, nontenured teachers may be given the opportunity to participate in the self-directed pathway in lieu of completing a professional development portfolio.

Interim Meeting

An interim report will be developed in conference with the teacher and administrator by January 15th. The teacher's progress toward meeting the district's Descriptors of Effective Teaching and learning goals (Portfolio) will be discussed and recorded and recommendations made.

Annual Evaluation Summary Report (AESR)

An Annual Evaluation Summary Report (AESR) will be developed in conference with the teacher and administrator by April 30th. The teacher's progress toward meeting the district's Descriptors of Effective Teaching and attainment of goals specified in the Professional Development Portfolio will be discussed. The annual evaluation summary report will include reflections on the teacher's progress, guidance toward continued growth, and a formal record of observations, participation in professional development activities, and recommendation on continuation of employment.

Self-Directed Professional Growth Pathway

This pathway provides possibilities and options for continued professional growth that will result in increased expertise and a deeper understanding of the teaching and learning process for experienced, tenured teachers. Demonstration of Descriptors of Effective Teaching is an ongoing process, and administrators have the continuous responsibility of monitoring excellence by using multiple alternative sources of data about daily practice that include, but are not limited to, formal and informal observation, student achievement, teacher interview, and student-parental feedback.

This pathway emphasizes continuous appraisal of performance, with a focus on self-assessment that leads to a planning process that is flexible, creative, and stimulating. Professional Growth Plans are developed, which focus on activities that connect to subject area, school, or district initiatives and, ultimately, to student learning. Staff members are encouraged to work collaboratively with a partner or team. The plan design may include learning activities for one-, two- or three-year periods. Participants may revise and/or expand their focus, dependent on learning experiences.

Possible areas of inquiry and/or investigation for professional growth plans could include, but are not to be restricted to:

Refinement of Current Practice

This area addresses the refinement of more complex teaching skills and strategies (e.g., questioning, motivation techniques, and small-group instruction) that the staff member is currently using in practice. This type of plan is generally individual, and short term in nature—one year.

Acquisition of New Skills

This area assumes access to resources to acquire and support new skills or knowledge, (i.e., integration of technology and brain-based strategies). This type of plan may be an individual or team endeavor, relates to teaching discipline and district goals, and may span one to three years.

Redesign and Restructuring

This area always requires additional resources, time, and district commitment. This is primarily a team endeavor, spans two to three years, and connects to building or district initiatives. The product would typically be a design that includes rationale for change, student outcomes, and changes in curriculum and instruction and evaluation plan.

Development of Curriculum and Program Goals

This area has three potential directions:

Deepening: Participants would generally address moving curriculum coverage to a "deeper level" (focusing on themes rather than sequences of facts). This endeavor may use an individual or team approach and generally spans one to three years.

Integrating: Participants would focus on developing integrated lessons and levels. This endeavor is generally done by teams and spans two to three years.

Engaging: Participants would develop materials and activities that focus on engaging students in the classroom, based on special needs, styles, and/or developmental stages. This may be an individual or team endeavor and spans one to three years.

Specific Student Outcomes and Assessment

This area addresses the development of new and/or alternative assessments that measure or describe student learning (standards-based assessment). This endeavor may use an individual or team approach and span one to three years.

Special Population/Equity—Opportunity to Learn

This area focuses on developing new or enhanced learning opportunities for special-needs students (i.e., gifted, at-risk, or special education). This may be an individual or group approach and span one to three years.

Possible strategies and/or activities for the learning plan could include, but would not be limited to, any combination of the following:

- action research
- coaching
- videotaping
- study groups
- mentoring
- college courses
- simulations
- shadowing experiences

- workshops and conferences
- visitation model schools
- lesson planning
- classroom observations
- teacher academies
- peer conferences
- professional dialogue
- electronic networking

Possible products could include, but would not be limited to:

- student portfolios
- videotapes of classes
- staff workshops
- case-study analysis
- student inventories
- published work

- curriculum units
- performance assessments
- reflective journals
- professional portfolios
- electronic portfolios

The collaborative process guides the development of the Professional Growth Plan. Initially, staff members will develop a draft of their plan. By November 1st, they will meet, and collaborate with, an administrator to refine and finalize this plan. Partners or team members will identify mutually convenient times to work on, and discuss, activities and experiences. Additionally, formal opportunity for professional staff to meet will be scheduled at least five times per school year, including a final celebration of learning. Administrators will meet mid-year with individuals or teams to discuss progress, strategies and activities to date, and identify next steps and additional resources needed to accomplish their learning focus. By April 15th, teacher(s) will complete a written reflection of the process to date that will serve as a focus for dialogue with the administrator at the end-of-year conference. The role of the administrator will be to facilitate the development of the plan, and to support and/or provide guidance throughout the process.

Annual Evaluation Summary Report (AESR)

An Annual Evaluation Summary Report (AESR) will be developed in conference with the teacher by June 15th. The administrator and teacher will address the ongoing performance of the teacher as it relates to the Descriptors of Effective Teaching. They will also discuss the Professional Growth Plan, including process, discoveries, professional activities, and related experiences, as well as future direction.

Teachers in the second pathway, therefore, do not receive any 60-minute observations. Administrators may always visit a classroom and spend some time there, but there is no requirement for a teacher who achieves all the descriptors of effective teaching to receive a full classroom observation. Instead, teachers in the second pathway work in self-selected teams of no more than five teachers, to work to complete a professional growth plan that is directly tied toward school and district goals. In other words, teams of teachers apply curriculum and professional development toward their own growth, and this plan focuses on collecting evidence of student achievement. The teams meet with one administrator at mid-term and at the end of the year, to discuss progress toward achieving their goal(s). A final evaluation is written for each teacher in the second pathway, based on notes taken from those meetings and the collection of student evidence of academic achievement.

Professional Assistance Pathway

This pathway provides a more structured and intensive mode of supervision for the tenured professional staff member who is not consistently demonstrating one or more of the fundamental competencies. A more formalized process characterizes this option. The administrator will direct the development of a plan of action that should ultimately result in the teacher's demonstration of the competencies specified.

Ideally, intensive supervision is characterized by recognition, on the part of the teacher and the administrator, that specifically directed assistance in identified areas will lead to success in the classroom. Observations and supervision in this Pathway will be formative and clinical.

Intensive supervision should be collaborative, but may also be directive. It is intended to provide the best likelihood for the attainment of competency and professional growth. It should maintain the supportive climate inherent in the supportive process for as long as possible, yet it may also become a summative, directed process that leads to further administrative action, which might ultimately result in withholding an increment and/or dismissal.

This Pathway Consists of Two Phases

Awareness Phase

In the awareness phase, the administrator identifies a problem relating to fundamental competencies that is characteristic of a teacher's performance, rather than an anomaly. Multiple alternative sources of data might include, but are not limited to, formal and informal observation, student achievement, teacher interview, and student and/or parental feedback. The administrator contacts the staff member in writing, makes him or her aware of the problem, collaboratively develops the means to resolve the problem, and schedules a time (not to exceed three months) to discuss a resolution. While the administrator and teacher attempt to resolve the problem, the teacher continues to work on the professional growth plan and remains in the self-directed pathway.

Professional Assistance

Based on documentation of lack of resolution of a problem relating to fundamental competencies, the staff member moves into the professional assistance phase that is based on an intensive supervision model.

After a meeting and discussion between the administrator and the teacher, a letter is sent to the teacher to formally notify him or her of placement in the Professional Assistance Pathway. A copy is forwarded to the superintendent and the personnel file. At this time, a mentor may also be assigned at the teacher's option.

Procedures

A conference is held between the teacher and the administrator to develop an assistance plan that includes a specific statement of problems relating to the Descriptors of Effective Teaching, as well as specific growth-promoting goals that are measurable, action-oriented, realistic, and time-bound. In addition, the plan will include strategies to be applied in achieving the goals, intended timelines for the strategic actions, and specific criteria for evaluating the successful completion of the plan.

Agreement will be reached between the teacher and the administrator on the necessary resources to accomplish the goals and objectives. A specific and detailed timeline will be worked out for the teacher and administrator to review progress. This should be in intervals of no longer than two weeks, with a final review scheduled within a calendar year.

During this time period, the administrator will conduct formal and informal observations and evaluations. The administrator will conduct a pre- and postconference, providing written feedback and specific suggestions for each formal observation. Ongoing verbal feedback is critical to this process.

Interim conferences will be scheduled at the mid-point in this process. The teacher and administrator will conduct a formal conference to review performance. The conference will be an analysis of performance and the degree of achievement of previously stated goals. A written evaluation will result from this review. The evaluation should be reviewed in a follow-up conference with the teacher. Copies of this document will be added by the teacher to the teacher's professional portfolio and sent by the administrator to the central office personnel file. Adjustments and refocusing of the plan can occur at any time during the year in response to teacher growth.

Annual Evaluation Summary Report (AESR)

The Annual Evaluation Summary Report (AESR) is a written summary report developed in conference by the teacher and administrator. It is performance-based and includes an assessment of attainment of goals and participation in professional development activities, as described in the Professional Assistance Plan. It also requires a reflection on the process by the staff member. Copies of this summative evaluation report will be forwarded by the administrator to the central office and placed in the teacher's personnel file. Having demonstrated successful achievement of the Professional Assistance Plan goals, a decision will be made regarding the appropriate supervision-evaluation pathway for the next school year. If the teacher has demonstrated progress toward, but not fulfillment of, the goals stated in the Professional Assistance Plan, then the administrator may recommend continuation in this Pathway for a specified period of time.

If it is determined that the teacher is not able to meet the district's professional standards, the administrator, in consultation with the superintendent, may make recommendations for the withholding of increment and/or dismissal. Withholding of increment and/or dismissal can only be acted on after the steps in the Professional Assistance Supervision Pathway have been implemented; however, the underlying assumption exists that teacher behaviors threatening the safety and welfare of students will result in immediate disciplinary action for any teacher.

This third pathway, therefore, is meant as a supportive step for tenured staff who, while in the second pathway, may fail in one or more of the Descriptors of Effective Teaching. It is neither a punitive measure nor a pathway destined for those teachers who may be dismissed. Instead, it is a pathway that enables a teacher who needs assistance, and an administrator, to draft a plan toward improvement. In this pathway, tenured teachers will receive classroom observations to demonstrate mastery of the Descriptors of Effective Teaching. This pathway provides a structured process to remediate a teacher toward regaining mastery of the Descriptors of Effective Teaching.

Overview of Supervision Evaluation Pathways

Descriptors of Effective Teaching: A Framework for Continuous Growth

- Planning and Preparation
- Classroom Environment

- Instruction
- Professional Responsibilities

Final Reflections

Understanding adult learners is key to a successful mentoring program. Just as teachers recognize the diverse learning needs of their students by understanding their learning styles, and how they develop over time, a school district needs to learn how adults learn best when developing their own mentoring program. For this reason alone, a key to mentoring excellence rests in creating ways for new teachers and mentors to engage in activities that employ dialogue and written reflection centered around student learning. The most effective mentors know best how to facilitate this reflection, how to guide the protégé toward self-assessment, and how to direct the protégé toward ongoing professional development and growth.

Maintaining trust, compassion, and a connection between the mentor and protégé are also integral to a successful program. While the mentor should not formally evaluate the new teacher, if a school district wants to build trust and retain its new teachers, it must also change the way it is evaluating and supervising its teachers. A differentiated evaluation system is necessary, in order to enhance professional practice for both beginning and experienced teachers.

A strong mentoring program can very well be the catalyst for creating a lifelong professional community of learners who focus on student achievement and the importance of building and maintaining effective relationships.

References

Barth, R. (2001). Teachers at the helm. *Education Week, 20*(24), 32–33, 48.

Bettleheim, B. (1989). *Uses of enchantment: The meaning and importance of fairy tales*. New York: Random House.

Boreen, J., Johnson, M., Niday, D., & Potts, J. (2000). *Mentoring beginning teachers*. York, ME: Stenhouse.

Danielson, C., & McGreal, T. (2000). *Teacher evaluation to enhance professional practice*. Alexandria, VA: Association for Supervision and Curriculum Development.

Evertson, C., & Smithey, M. (2000). Mentoring effects on protégés' classroom practice: An experimental field study. *Journal of Educational Research, 93*(5), 294–304.

Gold, Y. (1999). Beginning teacher support. In J. Sikula, T. Buttery, & E. Guyton (Eds.). *Handbook of research in teacher education* (2nd ed.). New York: Macmillan.

Tatum, B., & McWhorter, P. (Eds.). (1999). *Maybe not everything, but a whole lot you always wanted to know about mentoring. Teacher mentor: A dialogue for collaborate learning.* New York: Teachers College, Columbia University.
Zachary, L. (2000). *The mentor's guide.* San Francisco, CA: John Wiley & Sons.

For Consideration

1. Which characteristics of an effective protégé do you consider most important? Explain.
2. As demonstrated in this chapter, how can mentoring help to create partnerships among administration, the Board of Education, experienced teachers, and protégés?
3. What is a mentor?

Appendix

Descriptors of Professional Practice
Child Study Team Member

I. Management and Organization

Schedules time efficiently
- maintains calendar and log of planned activities
- attends required meetings

Provides professional services within established timelines
- mandated counseling is provided per Individualized Evaluation Plan (IEP)
- communicates with other professional staff providing related services

Evaluates students according to N.J.A.C. 6A: 14 requirements
- reevaluations are conducted within three years
- initial evaluations are completed within 60 days
- evaluations include student observations
- evaluations include parental input as required and/or appropriate

Facilitates development of the IEP for students
- insures all components of IEP are developed
- includes parents, student, and staff in IEP process
- insures IEP meets least restrictive mandate

Coordinates activities required upon student referral
- gathers and analyzes information available on student performance
- communicates with pertinent staff members
- facilitates decision-making process
- provides written decision regarding evaluation to parents and staff within timelines established

Arranges required services for students, as delineated in the IEP
- insures all related services are provided per IEP in the area of:
  - transportation
  - O.T., P.T., Speech
  - testing accommodations

Demonstrates effective collaboration with members of the Colleague Support Team (CST)
- plans evaluation procedures in consultation with colleagues
- decision making occurs as a collaborative process relative to determining eligibility and placement
- interaction with team members reflects a professional attitude

Reviews and revises the IEP, as required by N.J.A.C. 6A: 14 requirements
- conducts annual reviews per timelines established
- conducts triennial evaluations per timelines established
- plans IEP meetings as requested by parents or dictated by circumstances
- reviews and revises IEPs needed for new entrants within timelines established

Adheres to school and district procedures as well as policies established by way of federal and state law
- demonstrates adherence to all local policies and procedures in the course of their work
- adheres to N.J.A.C. 6A: 14 rules and regulations
- practice reflects conformance to Individuals with Disabilities Education Act (IDEA) guidelines

Arranges for utilization of consultants to meet timelines and N.J.A.C. 6A: 14 requirements
- plans in advance for use of consultants
- forwards consultant form to district office
- arranges consultant services
- advises Director of Special Education of circumstances not covered by N.J.A.C. 6A: 14 requirements

II. Case Management

Monitors student progress in a formative manner
- maintains communication on student cases with coordinating teacher and guidance counselor
- reviews progress reports and standardized testing information
- seeks teachers' input as needed to determine rate of progress

Consults with staff regarding student progress
- seeks out staff to discuss student progress
- requests staff input in writing
- includes pertinent staff in meetings as appropriate

Provides consultation to both regular and special education teachers
- recommends teaching and behavioral strategies to teaching staff

- shares pertinent information on student cases with staff as necessary to promote student growth

Provides counseling services to students and parent
- advises parents and students regarding availability of community services
- provides supportive counseling to students in a formative manner
- counsels parents relative to concerns which arise for student(s) in the school community context

Participates in the development and evaluation of goals and objectives for the IEP
- selects goals and objectives for the IEP as appropriate (i.e., counseling and transition)
- evaluates student progress toward specific goals and objectives
- facilitates the selection of goals and objectives for the overall academic program

Provides consultation services to the building administration
- advises building administration as needed regarding the individual needs or concerns of students with disabilities
- assists the building administration with schoolwide issues related to students with disabilities

Facilitates the planning for students' "transition" to adult roles
- includes "transition planning" as an element of the IEP
- ensures goals and objectives are developed in the area of transition to adult roles
- ensures linkages are developed with appropriate outside agencies in support of students in transition

Communicates effectively with all staff regarding the nature and needs of students with disabilities
- provides in-service periodically to assist staff in their work with students with disabilities
- communicates in person and in writing the needs of students for whom they case manage

Coordinates management of student cases with student's guidance counselor
- coordinates with guidance counselor during the scheduling process, annual reviews, reevaluations, and miscellaneous activities within the school or community context
- provides required scheduling input relative to IEP to guidance counselor

Coordinates management of students placed in out-of-district schools
- ensure all requirements are met per N.J.A.C. 6A: 14
- consult with school staff as required to facilitate success
- facilitate transcript development

III. Professionalism

Maintains a professional working relationship with both parents and students
- a positive rapport is evident in the working relationship
- CST member models respectful behavior
- written communications reflect a professional disposition

Demonstrates concern for the schoolwide community
- participation in schoolwide committees
- advisement in athletics and/or extracurricular activities
- demonstrates personal interest and participation in various activities
- demonstrates professional commitment

Demonstrates a commitment to the continuing development of skills associated with their specialty field and lifelong learning
- attends workshops, graduate courses, and/or district in-service
- demonstrates collegiality

Interacts appropriately with students and parents in all aspects of their work
- CST member conveys a positive regard for all students
- demonstrates a supportive role as case manager

Provides emergency interventions and crisis counseling services as may be needed
- intervene as requested
- demonstrate accepted standards for professional practices
- makes appropriate referrals
- follow up as necessary

Descriptors of Professional Practice

Educational Media Specialist

I. Management and Organization

Operates and supervises the school library or media center
- keeps calendar
- has procedures or routines
- maintains and assesses collection

Maintains a facility with an atmosphere conducive to learning
- updates technology—hardware and software
- has procedures or routines

Maintains a comprehensive and efficient system for cataloging all media center materials
- oversees cataloging, weeding, and inventory

Evaluates, selects, and requisitions new media center materials, and informs teachers and staff of new acquisitions
- publishes handouts or newsletter describing acquisitions

Supervises clerical, paid professional, and aide activities necessary to effective operation
- coordinate schedule
- assigns and monitors tasks

II. Instructional Consulting

Assists teachers in the selection of books and other instructional materials and makes media center materials available to supplement the instructional programs
- conducts training for teachers
- collaborates with staff

Plans with teachers regarding the use of the library media center in conjunction with student research assignments
- is knowledgeable about research sources
- identifies sources

Participates in curriculum development
- provides support for administration and teachers

III. Instruction

Instructs students and staff in the use of library media center resources, coordinates library skills instruction, and provides a sequential program of library skills instruction
- prepares lessons and materials
- monitors sequential skill development

Informally instructs students and staff in use of various types of materials and equipment
- acknowledges and reacts to student and staff needs
- provides appropriate tutorials and whole-group instruction

Presents and discusses materials with a class studying a particular topic at the request of the teacher
- prepares lessons
- coordinates with teachers

Instructs students in information retrieval skills and techniques necessary for independent research and lifelong learning
- prepares and delivers lessons and tutorials

IV. Professionalism

Demonstrates a concern for the schoolwide community
- attends meetings
- communicates with departments
- conferences with staff
- recognizes student interests
- reads, shares, and circulates materials of interest

Demonstrates a commitment to the development of library and technology skills and lifelong learning
- takes courses, attends seminars and workshops
- participates in professional activities
- conferences with other media specialists

Interacts appropriately with students beyond the confines of the classroom
- communicates in writing and by phone

Shows progress in completing professional growth requirements as agreed upon
- prepares and implements a yearly professional growth plan
- maintains a professional portfolio, if required

Stays current in the areas of librarianship, curriculum and technology, and attends professional organization meetings or seminars

- attends conferences and meetings
- reads appropriate material
- takes courses

Acts as liaison to sending district media specialists. Exchanges information on instruction, collection, development, technology, and so forth.

- attends meetings
- writes memos and news items
- does reports and analyses

Descriptors of Professional Practice
Guidance Counselor

I. Fundamental Competencies

The counselor:
- demonstrates knowledge of theory and techniques related to guidance and counseling
- interacts effectively and positively with students, staff, and parents
- uses time efficiently and effectively in carrying out responsibilities in his or her position
- communicates with families about the instructional program and individual student progress
- provides feedback in a timely manner
- disseminates information clearly in verbal and written forms
- prepares written recommendations, which reflect thoughtful and comprehensive understanding of the student
- adheres to school and district procedures and deadlines
- actively participates in self-directed pathway

II. Professional Responsibility

The counselor:
- continues professional development by demonstrating a commitment to the continuing development of counseling skills and acquiring guidance and career information
- demonstrates professional ethics and models professional behaviors
- adheres to school and district procedures and policies
- uses professional judgment as to when, where, and with whom to discuss student information
- works for harmonious relationships with others and fosters the building of a trusting environment
- projects a positive, cooperative attitude as a member of the student professional team
- actively participates in self-directed professional pathway

III. Counseling

The counselor:
- demonstrates knowledge of theory and techniques related to guidance and counseling
- knows each student's background and monitors the total development of the student
- helps students grow in the areas of academic, personal, social, and career development

- provides periodic counseling services to all students through individual and group counseling and guidance and addresses students' academic, personal, and vocational concerns
- prepares written recommendations, which reflect thoughtful and comprehensive understanding of the student
- acts as consultant to staff, CST, parents, students, community, in reference to students' growth, progress, and development

IV. Communication

The counselor:
- disseminates information clearly in verbal and written form
- communicates with families about the instructional program and individual student progress
- works with teachers and other staff members to familiarize them with the general range of services offered by the student personnel services department
- seeks, shares, and respects the ideas of other professional staff

V. Time Management and Organization

The counselor:
- uses procedures and routines which facilitate an effective guidance program
- follows through on all assignments without having to be reminded
- uses time efficiently and effectively in carrying out responsibilities in his or her position
- completes tasks, reports, and analyses in a timely fashion
- establishes and maintains a recordkeeping system specific to job role

Descriptors of Professional Practice

Nurse

I. Management and Organization

Reflects effective planning
- maintains calendar
- plans for activities
- maintains log, scheduling timetable, lists for follow-ups or referrals
- coordinates with school physician

Manages the health office effectively
- maintains student log
- has procedures and routines
- schedules appointments with students and staff
- meets students' concerns and problems

Evaluates the outcomes of the stated goals, as well as those which emerge as the year unfolds
- assesses practice and procedures
- reviews completion of annual programs

Acts as a decision maker who takes charge of the program and makes changes as the year proceeds
- makes program recommendations as necessary
- meets with appropriate personnel and recommends needed changes in the program

Develops and maintains a health records system
- reviews new school entrants
- keeps current documentation regarding medication, charting, gym restrictions, and self-medication records
- uses state health forms

Adheres to school and district procedures and deadlines
- maintains accurate records
- meets appropriate deadlines

II. Nursing

Demonstrates respect for students and their problems
- has positive interactions with students when discussing students' health issues and validating their concerns
- creates a nurturing environment

- encourages further participation of students by questioning and listening

Reflects an in-depth understanding of the medical problems faced by high school students
- demonstrates ability to explain medical concepts
- recognizes students health issues and how they may affect classroom learning
- demonstrates knowledge and experience beyond the textbook
- demonstrates ability to respond to students' questions and inquiries

Implements pertinent laws and regulations
- follows school nursing state guidelines
- conducts workshops as mandated
- complies with state and federal regulations and submits reports as required

Implements board policy relative to drugs, alcohol, medication, physical exams, and special education
- maintains/reviews/documents/records
- completes required screenings

Practices confidentiality in all health areas
- talks to students privately as needed
- maintains records and health information in a confidential manner

Knows about, chooses from, and implements appropriate approaches to dealing with students, parents, coaches, teachers, and other health professionals
- engages in ongoing professional development activities
- dialogues with other school nurses

Maintains a mutually respectful environment
- models respectful behaviors
- uses verbal and nonverbal language that reflects acceptance
- creates a climate in which students feel comfortable discussing their medical issues
- interacts with students at appropriate level

III. Professionalism

Maintains positive communication with staff, parents, school physicians, and community health professionals
- attends meetings
- communicates in writing and by phone
- participates in consultations and agency referrals

Projects a positive image which encourages cooperation within the staff
- accommodates teacher requests

- provides staff feedback
- uses diplomacy in interactions

Actively demonstrates concern for the schoolwide community
- interacts with parents
- conferences with staff
- recognizes various student interests
- reads, shares, and circulates materials of interest
- communicates with staff regarding student health needs as appropriate

Demonstrates a commitment to the continuing development of nursing skills and lifelong learning
- takes courses, attends seminars and workshops
- participates in professional activities
- conferences with other school nurses

Interacts appropriately with students beyond the confines of the classroom
- acknowledges students' actions in and out of the classroom
- maintains positive posture with all students

Descriptors of Professional Practice
Speech and Language Pathologist

I. Management and Organization

Schedules time efficiently
- maintains calendar or log of planned activities
- attends required meetings

Provides professional services within established timelines
- provides speech services per IEP requirements
- conducts speech evaluations in a timely manner

Evaluates students according to N.J.A.C. 6A: 14 requirements
- completes initial evaluations within 60 days
- conducts reevaluations within three years
- evaluations include student observations
- evaluations include parental input as required and/or appropriate

Facilitates development of the IEP for speech
- insures all components of IEP are developed for speech and language services
- includes parents, student, and staff in IEP process
- insures IEP meets least restrictive mandate

Coordinates activities required upon student referral
- gathers and analyzes information available on student performance
- communicates with pertinent staff members
- facilitates decision-making process
- provides written decision regarding evaluation to parents and staff within timelines established

Arranges required speech and language services for students, as delineated in the IEP
- coordinates schedule of speech services with pertinent staff
- commences speech services per IEP

Demonstrates effective collaboration with members of the CST and teaching staff
- plans evaluation procedures in consultation with colleagues
- decision making occurs as a collaborative process relative to determining evaluation plan, eligibility, and placement
- interaction with team members and teaching staff reflects a professional attitude

Reviews and revises the IEP speech component as required by N.J.A.C. 6A: 14
requirements
- conducts annual reviews per timelines established
- conducts triennial evaluations per timelines established
- plans IEP meetings as requested by parents or dictated by circumstances
- reviews and revises IEP needed for new entrants within timelines established
- evaluates student progress in a formative manner
- seeks input from staff regarding students' needs

Adheres to school and district procedures, as well as policies established by way
of federal and state law
- demonstrates adherence to all local policies and procedures in the course
of their work
- adheres to N.J.A.C. 6A: 14 rules and regulations
- practice reflects conformance to IDEA guidelines

Arranges for utilization of consultants to meet timelines and N.J.A.C. 6A: 14
requirements
- plans in advance for use of consultants
- forwards consultant form to district office
- arranges consultant services
- advises Director of Special Education of circumstances not covered by
N.J.A.C. 6A: 14 requirements

II. Speech and Language Instruction

Provision of services reflects effective planning
- uses time for instruction efficiently
- has evidence of a written plan
- demonstrates correlation between IEP and student activities

Methodology is appropriate to students' needs and supported by research
- utilizes methods based upon professional speech evaluations, as well as
parental and staff input
- methodology considers the impact of disabilities other than speech
- methods insure application of skills taught

Instructional materials selected by Speech Language Pathology (SLP) reflect the
needs of the student, as delineated in the IEP
- uses materials which enhance functional application
- uses materials which are current, relevant, and motivating to the student
- provides a variety of activities to meet IEP goals and objectives

Communicates to students' expectations, which are challenging and appropriate
- provides a high level of structure for unit and/or daily lessons
- provides frequent feedback for students
- assesses student progress in a formative manner
- encourages and requires student application of skills under development

Demonstrates respect for students and their learning
- interacts positively with students throughout instructional process
- recognizes accomplishments of students
- encourages a high level of participation

Evaluates outcomes of instruction as related to IEP goals and objectives
- incorporates alternative assessments
- seeks parental input on student progress
- seeks staff input on student progress and applications

Communicates the importance of the skills taught to the students
- relates the relevancy of skills to daily living skills
- relates the significance of the skills with conviction and enthusiasm

III. Professionalism

Maintains a professional working relationship with both parents and students
- demonstrates positive rapport in the working relationship
- models respectful behavior
- written communications reflect a professional disposition

Demonstrates concern for the schoolwide community
- participates in schoolwide committees
- advises in athletics and/or extra curricular activities
- demonstrates personal interest and participates in various activities
- demonstrates professional commitment

Demonstrates a commitment to the continuing development of skills associated with their specialty field and lifelong learning
- attends workshops, graduate courses, and/or district in-service
- demonstrates collegiality

Interacts appropriately with students and parents in all aspects of their work
- conveys a positive regard for all students
- demonstrates a supportive role as case manager

Contributes to the professional interaction during IEP meetings
- topics initiated are professional contributions intended to solve problems or otherwise assist in meeting the goals of the meeting

- contributions are within the SLP's area of expertise

Provides leadership in the areas of speech and language development for students with disabilities
- recommends improvements to services offered district students
- disseminates information to professional staff regarding speech- and language-related disabilities

Descriptors of Professional Practice

Substance Awareness Coordinator

I. Management, Organization, and Planning

Assists in the development of the Drug Free Schools and Communities Act (DFSCA) grant application
- provides evaluation data and demographic information for application
- gathers evaluation data on services provided during school year
- provides information necessary to plan activities and build the budget

Develops and implements programs for assisting students at-risk
- organizes and implements a counseling program for students at-risk
- plans and implements programs for at-risk youth, which build self-esteem and improves decision-making skills
- provides a reentry counseling program for students returning from rehabilitation centers

Participates in the implementation of Board policy upon identification of student substance abuse–related issues
- provides information to students and parents regarding rehabilitation centers as appropriate

Develops or revises procedures for referral of students affected by substance abuse
- obtains input from staff regarding efficacy of procedures developed
- recommends in writing any changes to procedures or Board policy to administration

Develops and implements educational programs for parents focusing on substance-abuse issues
- plans and implements informational meetings for parents relative to substance-abuse prevention
- provides written information for parents at evening functions (i.e., back-to-school nights, curriculum nights, and so forth)

Assists with the development and implementation of a Grades 9–12 curriculum on alcohol- and drug-abuse prevention
- conducts informal evaluation of health curriculum on topics related to area of specialty
- assists health teachers in implementing curriculum in role of substance-abuse expert

- recommends those areas of health curriculum requiring evaluation and/or revision
- assists with the evaluation of staff needs for in-service programs

II. Counseling

Provides counseling services to students identified as at-risk and those returning from treatment
- maintains a log of counseling activities
- develops confidential student lists
- provides counseling services as needed by student(s)

III. Communication

Demonstrates skills and written communication
- correspondence

Interacts appropriately with students, using knowledge of adolescent development and behavior patterns
- observations of counseling intervention
- observations during student-parent meetings

Strives to gain parents' interest, confidence, and respect by being a good listener and handling difficult situations with objectivity
- observations during parent meetings
- feedback from colleagues

Initiates communication with parents about student performance and/or behavior where appropriate
- case notes
- parental feedback

Actively participates in student/teacher/parent conferences relating to substance-abuse issues
- shares community resources
- utilizes problem-solving techniques

Consults with, and makes referrals to, agencies, other staff members or specialists, and other appropriate community resources
- conducts outreach to maintain up-to-date list of resources
- observation of professional level of interaction with students and parents
- observation of professional staff interactions
- parents receive information relating to resources available
- updates professional staff on community resources available

Strives to establish rapport with students, parents, and school staff
- observation of student-parent interactions
- observation of staff interactions

Provides inservice to the faculty on topics related to substance abuse
- updates appropriate staff on developments in specialty area
- trains the general faculty on specific substance-abuse topics as requested

Evaluates student progress and communicates their needs to appropriate Pupil Assistance Committee (PAC) members and/or administration
- communicates with administration and staff

IV. Professionalism

Provides leadership in the areas of identification, assessment, and service provision for students affected by substance abuse
- recommends improvements to services offered to district students
- recommends changes to policy and procedures at building and district levels

Maintains a positive working relationship with students, parents, and professional staff
- observations of student-parent interactions
- consultation with professional staff is evident

Demonstrates concern for the schoolwide community
- participates activities designed to promote positive school and community relations (i.e., extracurricular, special school events, or committee work)

Demonstrates a commitment to the continuing development of skills associated with counseling and substance abuse
- reads, shares information, and takes courses
- attends seminars or workshops

Contributes to the professional interaction during Pupil Assistance Committee (PAC) meetings
- effective problem-solving techniques observed

Demonstrates professional ethics and models professional behaviors
- observation in school
- observation at school events
- observation at parent conferences

Maintains student/counselor/family confidentiality as is deemed professionally appropriate
- PAC processes
- referral processes
- counseling processes

West Morris Regional High School District
Chester, New Jersey

❏ WMM   ❏ WMC
OBSERVATION FORM

Name _____ Administrator _____

Class _____ Date _____

Descriptors of Effective Teaching	
Planning and Preperation The Teacher: • demonstrates content knowledge • designs written plans that reflect goals and objectives of the curriculum • frequently evaluates outcomes of instruction for the achievement of stated goals • knows about, chooses from, and implements appropriate approaches to teaching	**Instruction** The Teacher: • communicates to students clearly and accurately • uses a variety of questioning and discussion techniques • engages students in learning • provides meaningful feedback to students
Classroom Environment The Teacher: • establishes a culture for learning • fosters a code of mutual respect and models respectful behavior • manages instructional time efficiently • manages student standards of conduct	**Professional Responsibility** The Teacher: • articulates principal goals of instructional practice, which promotes student learning • adheres to school and district procedures and deadlines • communicates with families about the instructional program and individual students • actively demonstrates concern for the schoolwide community • demonstrates a commitment to the continuing development of teaching skills and lifelong learning

The Descriptors of Effective Teaching are the basis for the following comments:

1. Planning and Preparation _____

_____

_____

_____

_____

2. Classroom Environment _____

_____

_____

_____

_____

3. Instruction _____

_____

_____

_____

_____

4. Professional Responsibilities _____

_____

_____

_____

_____

5. Recommendations _____

_____

_____

_____

_____   _____

Staff Member   Date   Administrator   Date

WEST MORRIS REGIONAL HIGH SCHOOL DISTRICT

Chester, New Jersey

❑ WMM   ❑ WMC
INTERIM REPORT FORM

Direct Supervision Evaluation Pathway

Name_____   Administrators_____

Date_____

Progress on Descriptors of Effective Teaching:

1. Planning and Preparation _____

_____

_____

_____

_____

2. Classroom Environment _____

_____

_____

_____

_____

3. Instruction _____

_____

_____

_____

_____

4. Professional Responsibilities _____

_____

_____

_____

_____

Progress on Professional Development Portfolio _____

_____

_____

_____

_____

5. Recommendations _____

_____

_____

_____

                                    _____

_____   _____
Teacher   Date   Administrators   Date

WEST MORRIS REGIONAL HIGH SCHOOL DISTRICT

Chester, New Jersey

PROFESSIONAL DEVELOPMENT PORTFOLIO
Directive Pathway

Teacher   School

_____

_____

Learning Focus: _____

_____

_____

Focus is related to the following Descriptors of Effective Teaching:

_____

_____

_____

Focus is related to the following professional development standards:

_____ Content knowledge	_____ Assessment of student learning	
_____ Student needs	_____ Assessment of practice/program	
_____ Teaching skills	_____ School culture	
_____ Research/best practice	_____ Parent/community relationships	
_____ Integration of new learning		

Learning Plans—Proposed Strategies/Activities to address focus: _____

_____

_____

_____

Projected Products: _____

_____

_____

_____

Resources Required: _____

_____

_____

_____

Impact on Student Learning: _____

_____

_____

_____

Portfolio Partner(s): _____

_____

_____

_____

Ongoing Professional Development Activities

Beyond your specific activities related to identified focus, we recognize that you often participate in professional development activities or events related to overall school and district goals. Please indicate those areas and activities that are relevant to you and have not been included under your specific focus.

Additional areas of professional development related to school and district goals:

_____ Personal development planning process

_____ Curriculum alignment and development

_____ Technology applications and integration

_____ Interdisciplinary curriculum

_____ International Baccalaureate program

_____ Study skills infusion

_____ Needs of at-risk students

_____ Student participation within the school and community

_____ Facilities planning

_____ Supervision/Evaluation Initiative

_____ Safe and secure school environment

_____ Multiple methods of assessment

_____ Professional development planning

_____ Support systems for new teachers

_____ Content-specific knowledge/ pedagogy

Proposed events and activities to address school and district goals, including participation in or membership on:

_____ Delayed opening options	_____ Curriculum development project
_____ Institutes/seminars	_____ Project teams
_____ After-school courses	_____ District committees
_____ Discussion groups	_____ Mentoring
_____ Presentations	

_____   _____
Teacher   Date   Administrators   Date

EST MORRIS REGIONAL HIGH SCHOOL DISTRICT

Chester, New Jersey

❑ WMM   ❑ WMC

ANNUAL EVALUATION SUMMARY REPORT

Self-Directed Pathway

Name _____ Discipline _____

Administrator _____ Date _____

Descriptors of Effective Teaching/Counseling/Professional Practice: _____

_____

_____

_____

Professional Growth Plan Status: (include topic, focus question, experience, learn-

ing, and products) _____

_____

_____

_____

Professional Development Activities: (include type and hours) _____

_____

_____

_____

Future Directions: _____

_____

_____

_____

Administrator Comments: _____

_____

_____

_____

Staff Member Comments: _____

_____

_____

_____

Staff Member	Date	Administrators	Date

Index

About the Authors

Dr. Alyce Hunter

Alyce Hunter has been a teacher and administrator in New Jersey for 24 years. She has served as a middle school teacher, high school teacher, middles school administrator, high school administrator, and district administrator. Currently she is Director of Staff Development for the West Morris Regional High School District in Chester, NJ. Her duties include extensive supervision and evaluation of staff performance. Also she oversees a comprehensive mentoring program that unites veteran staff and new teachers. Dr. Hunter has taught at the graduate level at Wagner College School of Education for the past ten years. She has published numerous articles and two other books on educational topics. Dr. Hunter received a Fulbright Fellowship to study in Japan and two Korea Studies Fellowships. She received her doctorate in Foundations of Education from Lehigh University in 1996.

Dr. Henry Kiernan

With 31 years of educational experience as a teacher and administrator in New Jersey schools, Henry Kiernan is currently the Superintendent for the West Morris Regional High School District in Chester, NJ. He served as editor of The English Leadership Quarterly from 1994 to 2001. He has received awards from the New Jersey ASCD and the American School Board Journal for outstanding work in curriculum. His doctoral dissertation received the outstanding dissertation award from the National Staff Development Council. Currently, Dr. Kiernan is chair of the National Council for History Education. He received his doctorate in education from Rutgers University. He is the recipient of three Fulbright Fellowships to the People's Republic of China, Japan, and Germany. Dr. Kiernan has published numerous articles in educational journals and in scholarly history periodicals.

Maribeth Edmunds is currently the Director of Professional Development at the South Brunswick Public School District in Monmouth Junction, New Jersey. She developed and coordinated the district's Teacher Mentor Program that has been recognized as a model mentoring program by New Jersey's State Department of Education. Over the last five years, she has trained over 300 teachers to serve as mentors to novice teachers who are new to the profession. In addition, she serves on the 2004 Mentor Task Force for the Department of Education.

Dr. Judith A. Ferguson is managing partner of Centennium Consultants. LLC and is also Senior Associate with the superintendent search firm of Hazard, Young, Attea, and Associates, Ltd. She served in several leadership roles at the state and national levels including President of the New Jersey Association of School Administrators and Director on the Board of the Horace Mann League. As Senior Fellow for the New Jersey Citizens for Better Schools, Dr. Ferguson planned and administered leadership development programs for new and future superintendents and aspiring principals and chaired a major meeting on the crisis in school district leadership.

Nancy Hennessy has worked as a teacher, administrator, and consultant in both regular and special education. She holds an undergraduate degree in psychology, a graduate degree in special education and has completed advanced studies in administration. She has developed teacher training programs that have been presented on both state and national levels. She is currently the President of the International Dyslexia Association, serves on the National Joint Committee for Learning Disabilities and is a member of Recording for the Blind & Dyslexic's National Advisory Council. She is presently working as an educational consultant and is also an adjunct instructor at Fairleigh Dickinson University in Teaneck, New Jersey.

Ted Scott Henson is a retired thirty-four year veteran of education in North Carolina. He received his undergraduate and Masters Degrees from Campbell University and his Doctorate from Western Carolina University. He taught fifth grade for twenty-one years before moving to work at the central office level and finally to the university. Most recently, he was a Center Fellow for the North Carolina Center for the Advancement of Teaching in Cullowhee, North Carolina. He now does consulting work for the North Carolina Partnership for Excellence and several local school systems.

John R. Maitino, Professor of English and Coordinator of English Education at California State Polytechnic University Pomona, teaches courses in literature, methods of teaching English, and film; has published articles on "gender in literature," "improving teaching through the use of student evaluations of classroom teacher," "mentoring;" book reviews on composition texts. He coedited a book of essays, *Teaching American Ethnic Literature: 19 Essays* (University of New Mexico Press, 1996); and has presented widely across the United States on ethnic literature, multicultural literature, teaching, and mentoring.

∞

Ronald T. Sion has published a variety of scholarly articles, short stories, and poems as well as a book examining the novels of Aldous Huxley. As an educator, he has taught English on both the high school and college level for over twenty-two years. He currently teaches full time at Cranston High School East in Cranston, Rhode Island, and adjunct at the Rhode Island School of Design. His Ph.D. from Salve Regina University is in Modern Literature.

∞

Todd Toriello is a 2000 graduate from Lafayette College with a dual major in English and Government and Law. Following graduation, he completed a Maters program in English Education at Teachers College, Columbia University. Mr. Toriello is entering his fourth year of teaching English and is presently pursuing a second Masters degree in Administration/Supervision at Montclair State University.